TECHNICAL REPORT

Ambivalent Allies?

A Study of South Korean Attitudes Toward the U.S.

ERIC V. LARSON, NORMAN D. LEVIN
with SEONHAE BAIK, BOGDAN SAVYCH

TR-141-SRF

March 2004

Supported by the Smith Richardson Foundation

Approved for public release; distribution unlimited

RAND
CORPORATION

This research in the public interest was supported by the Smith Richardson Foundation and by the RAND Corporation, using discretionary funds made possible by the generosity of RAND's donors, the fees earned on client-funded research, and independent research and development (IR&D) funds provided by the Department of Defense.

Library of Congress Cataloging-in-Publication Data

Larson, Eric V. (Eric Victor), 1957-
    Ambivalent allies? : a study of South Korean attitudes toward the U.S. / Eric V. Larson, Norman D. Levin ; with Seonhae Baik, Bogdan Savych.
        p. cm.
    "TR-141."
    Includes bibliographical references.
    ISBN 0-8330-3584-3 (alk. paper)
    1. United States—Relations—Korea (South) 2. Korea (South)—Relations—United States. 3. Anti-Americanism—Korea (South) 4. United States—Foreign public opinion, Korean. 5. Public opinion—Korea (South) I. Larson, Eric V. (Eric Victor), 1957– II. Levin, Norman D. III. Baik, Seonhae. IV. Savych, Bogdan. V. Title.

E183.8.K6L37 2004
327.5195073'09'0511—dc22

                                                                          2004004736

The RAND Corporation is a nonprofit research organization providing objective analysis and effective solutions that address the challenges facing the public and private sectors around the world. RAND's publications do not necessarily reflect the opinions of its research clients and sponsors.

RAND® is a registered trademark.

Published 2004 by the RAND Corporation
1700 Main Street, P.O. Box 2138, Santa Monica, CA 90407-2138
1200 South Hayes Street, Arlington, VA 22202-5050
201 North Craig Street, Suite 202, Pittsburgh, PA 15213-1516
RAND URL: http://www.rand.org/
To order RAND documents or to obtain additional information, contact
Distribution Services: Telephone: (310) 451-7002;
Fax: (310) 451-6915; Email: order@rand.org

Preface

This is the final report of a RAND Corporation study of South Korean attitudes toward the United States that aimed to assess three key research questions:

(1) What are the trends in South Koreans' attitudes toward the United States and is the conventional wisdom that they recently have deteriorated correct?

(2) What are the sources of South Korean attitudes toward the United States, and what are their trends over time?

(3) What are the implications of these trends for U.S. policy toward Korea and larger security interests?

The study constituted an exhaustive effort to compile and analyze public opinion data on South Korean attitudes toward the United States, and a historical analysis of selected periods in U.S.-South Korean relations during the past decade which also sought to identify the sources of anti-U.S. attitudes.

Two working papers provide additional details on the data and analysis. They are

Seonhae Baik and Eric Larson, "South Korean Attitudes Toward the U.S.: Public Opinion Data," forthcoming.

Bogdan Savych and Eric Larson, "South Korean Attitudes Toward the U.S.: Statistical Modeling Results," forthcoming.

Interested readers can request these papers via e-mail from Eric Larson at larson@rand.org.

The study is likely to be of greatest interest to policymakers and scholars concerned with U.S.-South Korean relations and to those responsible for the development of public diplomacy programs. The research was sponsored through a generous grant from the Smith Richardson Foundation and RAND corporate funds, and was conducted in RAND's Center for Asia Pacific Policy (CAPP).

Center for Asia Pacific Policy (CAPP)

This research project was conducted under the auspices of the RAND Center for Asia-Pacific Policy (CAPP), which aims to improve public policy by providing decision makers and the public with rigorous, objective research on critical policy issues affecting Asia and U.S.-Asia relations. CAPP is part of RAND's National Security Research Division (NSRD). NSRD conducts research and analysis for a broad range of clients including the U.S. Department of Defense, the intelligence community, allied foreign governments, and foundations.

This technical report also results from RAND's continuing program of self-sponsored independent research. Support for such research is provided, in part, by donors and by the independent research and development provisions of RAND's contracts for the operation of its U.S. Department of Defense federally funded research and development centers.

For more information on RAND's Center for Asia Pacific Policy, contact the Director, Nina Hachigian. She can be reached by e-mail at Nina_Hachigian@rand.org; by phone at 310-393-0411, extension 6030; or by mail at RAND, 1700 Main Street, Santa Monica, California 90407-2138. More information about RAND is available at www.rand.org.

The RAND Corporation Quality Assurance Process

Peer review is an integral part of all RAND research projects. Prior to publication, this document, as with all documents in the RAND technical report series, was subject to a quality assurance process to ensure that the research meets several standards, including the following: The problem is well formulated; the research approach is well designed and well executed; the data and assumptions are sound; the findings are useful and advance knowledge; the implications and recommendations follow logically from the findings and are explained thoroughly; the documentation is accurate, understandable, cogent, and temperate in tone; the research demonstrates understanding of related previous studies; and the research is relevant, objective, independent, and balanced. Peer review is conducted by research professionals who were not members of the project team.

RAND routinely reviews and refines its quality assurance process and also conducts periodic external and internal reviews of the quality of its body of work. For additional details regarding the RAND quality assurance process, visit http://www.rand.org/standards/.

Contents

Preface iii

Figures ix

Tables xi

Summary xiii

Acknowledgments...xix

Acronyms. xxi

1. INTRODUCTION 1
   Approach..3
   Organization of This Report 5

2. THE PAST AS PROLOGUE...7
   Korea's Historic Experience 7
   Transition to the 1990s 12
   The Nuclear Crisis (1992–1996)...14
   The Inter-Korean Summit (2000–2002) 27
   History, the 1990s, and Factors Driving Korean Attitudes Toward
       the U.S..38

3. KEY TRENDS IN SOUTH KOREAN ATTITUDES TOWARD
   THE UNITED STATES 42
   Attitudes Toward the United States..42
   Attitudes Regarding U.S.-South Korean Relations............................48
   Attitudes Regarding Americans 50
   Attitudes Regarding the Alliance and the U.S. Military Presence 51
   How Do South Koreans' Attitudes Toward the U.S. Compare With
       Those Toward Other Nations?...59
   Chapter Conclusions 64

4. THE SOURCES OF SOUTH KOREAN ATTITUDES TOWARD
   THE U.S..66
   Many Views of the U.S., and Where the Problems Lie 66
   The Dynamics of Past Downturns in Favorable Sentiment.................73
   A Model of South Korean Attitudes Toward the U.S. 77
   Predictions of the Model 88
   Individual-Level Lenses..90
   Societal Influences 109
   Chapter Conclusions 118

5. IMPLICATIONS, RECOMMENDATIONS, CONCLUSIONS.............120
   Implications for the U.S...120
   Recommendations...122
   Conclusions 123

Bibliography 125

Figures

2.1 A Model of Influences on South Korean Attitudes Toward the U.S. 39

3.1 Percentage Mentioning U.S. as Most Liked Country 43

3.2 Percentage Mentioning U.S. as Most Disliked Country 44

3.3 Trends in Attitudes Toward the U.S., 1988–2003 45

3.4 Attitudes Toward the U.S., 1988–2003 47

3.5 Opinion on the State of U.S.-Korean Relations, 1988–2001 48

3.6 Opinion on the State of U.S.-Korean Relations, 1988–2001 49

3.7 Attitudes Toward Maintaining the Alliance After Reunification, 1997–2001 51

3.8 Importance of American Forces for Protecting Korea's Security, 1988–2001 53

3.9 Importance of American Forces for Protecting Korea's Security, 1988–2001 54

3.10 Attitudes Toward a U.S. Withdrawal, 1988–1996 56

3.11 Attitudes Toward a U.S. Withdrawal, 1990–2003 56

3.12 Favorable Sentiment Toward the U.S., China, and Japan, 1988–2001 63

4.1 Reason for Differences Between the U.S. and South Korea, August 2002 71

4.2 Reasons for Unfavorable View of the United States, August 2002 73

4.3 Model of South Korean Attitudes Toward the United States 79

4.4 Danger of a North Korean Attack In the Next Three Years, 1988–1999 82

4.5 Danger of a North Korean Attack In the Next Three Years, 1988–1999 82

4.6 Danger of Attack If Economic Sanctions Are Imposed, 1994–1995 .. 83

4.7 Expectations Regarding Reunification 87

4.8 Percentage Unfavorable by Age in State Department Polling, 1998–2001 92

4.9 Views of Threat to South Korea by Age 93

4.10 Country Posing the Greatest Threat to Korea, by Age 94

4.11 Percentage Liking and Disliking the U.S. by Education, July 1991 .. 96

4.12 Countries Identified by University Students as the Greatest Threat, April 1993 97

4.13 Percentage Favorable by Education, 9/93, 9/94, and 2/03 98

4.14 Percentage Unfavorable by Education, 9/93, 9/94/, and 2/03 99

4.15 Korean Average Daily Media Consumption, 1996–2000 101

4.16 Credibility of Newspaper and Television Broadcast Media 101

4.17 Major Korean Newspaper Reporting on the U.S., North Korea, and Reunification, 1990–2002 113

4.18 Selected Topics in Major Korean Newspaper Reporting on the
      U.S., 1990–2002 114
4.19 Selected Topics in Major Korean Newspaper Reporting on North
      Korea, 1990–2002 114

Tables

3.1 Comparison of South Korean Attitudes Toward the U.S. and Americans 50

3.2 Reasons For and Against U.S. Military Forces in South Korea, June 2000 58

3.3 Reasons For and Against U.S. Military Forces in South Korea, March 2002 59

3.4 Koreans' Views on Best Descriptions of U.S., Japan, and China, November 1999 60

3.5 Countries Most Liked by South Koreans, 1994–2003 61

3.6 Countries Most Disliked by South Koreans, 1994–2003 62

4.1 Koreans and Americans Views of Statements Best Describing the U.S., November 1999 67

4.2 Biggest Problems in U.S.-South Korean Relations, January and September 2000 68

4.3 Reasons for Having a Less Favorable Impression of the United States, February 2002 69

4.4 Main Reasons Some People Dislike the U.S., July 2002 70

4.5 Reasons People Dislike the United States, September 2003 70

4.6 South Korean and American Attitudes on Key Security Issues 72

4.7 Favorable and Unfavorable Sentiment Toward the United States, February 2002 75

4.8 Cross-Tabulation of Favorable Attitude Toward U.S. and Belief That North Korea Is a Threat to Stability 84

4.9 South Koreans' Evaluation of the Credibility of the U.S. Security Commitment 86

4.10 Views on the Possibility of Reunification, September 2003 88

4.11 Age Group Analysis of Unfavorable Opinion of U.S. 1991–2002 94

4.12 Cohort Analysis of Change in Unfavorable Opinion 1991–2002 95

4.13 Main Media Source for News, September 2003 102

4.14 Demographics of Online Survey at Pomdaewi Dissident Website . 104

4.15 Online Survey at Dissident Website: Attitudes Toward Arresting Pomdaewi 105

4.16 Cross-Tabulation of Favorability and Belief That U.S. Takes Other Nation's Interests Into Account, ... 106

4.17 Cross-Tabulation of Favorability and Belief That Culture Is Superior 107

4.18 Attitudes Toward U.S., China, and Japan Before and After June 2000 Korean Summit 108

4.19 Favorability of Attitudes Toward the U.S. by Geography, September 1993, September 1994, and February 2002 109

4.20 Next-Generation Leaders' Opinions on the Beneficiary of the Bilateral Relationship 111

4.21 The Beneficiary of the U.S. Military Forces in Korea 112

Summary

An increase in expressions of anti-American sentiment among South Koreans led, in the spring and summer of 2002, to heightened concern among many observers of South Korea (the Republic of Korea, or ROK) that a pillar of the U.S.-South Korean alliance—a strong belief among South Koreans in the continued importance of the U.S.-ROK alliance and an equally strong commitment to its continuation—might be in jeopardy.

This study's focus on favorable and unfavorable sentiment toward the U.S. within the South Korean mass public does not in any way challenge the proposition that most South Korean political and military leaders—as stewards of a now 50-year alliance with the U.S.—remain committed to a healthy and strong bilateral relationship with the U.S. The extent to which ordinary South Koreans may be less committed, however, is of obvious policy interest both to the U.S. and to them as well, because democratic theory—and historical experience—suggest that leadership often is needed to build and sustain support for contentious policies, and that public support is needed to sustain policies over the long run.

The RAND Corporation conducted an empirical study of the matter, addressing three key policy-relevant questions:

(1) What are the trends in South Koreans' attitudes toward the United States and is the conventional wisdom that they recently have deteriorated correct?

(2) What are the sources of South Korean attitudes toward the U.S., and what are their trends over time?

(3) What are the implications of these trends for U.S. policy toward Korea and larger security interests?

To address these questions, we conducted a qualitative analysis of the historical context for South Koreans' attitudes toward the U.S., and quantitative analyses of the available public opinion data on the matter.

A Recent Downturn in Favorable Sentiment Toward the U.S.

Our research demonstrates that there is strong evidence of a recent downturn in favorable sentiment toward the U.S. among South Koreans but also evidence of a more recent recovery. This downturn represented a departure from a generally favorable trend in South Koreans' views toward the U.S. since the early 1990s—on average, support was higher in the 1996–2001 period than in the 1990–1995 period that preceded it.

Favorable sentiment toward the U.S. plummeted in late February 2002 in reaction to an incident in which a South Korean speed skater lost the Olympic gold medal to an American. It then rose in the summer of 2002 but bottomed out again in December 2002, following the acquittal of two U.S. soldiers whose armored vehicle accidentally killed two South Korean schoolgirls.

The candlelight vigils and other public expressions of unfavorable sentiment toward the U.S. that occurred during this period tapered off after South Korean leaders indicated that such expressions were inimical to South Korea's interest in preserving its alliance with the U.S., and that they therefore should cease. Although expressions of unfavorable sentiment flared again at the time of the U.S. war with Iraq, they abated thereafter, and a feared resurgence of anti-American sentiment on the first anniversary of the June 2002 deaths of the school girls failed to materialize.

Moreover, many measures of sentiment toward the U.S.—attitudes toward the alliance, for example, and toward Americans—have remained strongly positive throughout the period.

The Sources of South Korean Attitudes Toward the U.S.

There are many sources of attitudes toward the U.S. among South Koreans.

Our qualitative historical analysis identified a number of key incidents and sources that have shaped South Korean attitudes toward the U.S. over the last decade: historical residue, U.S. and ROK leadership actions taken and not taken, the ROK's security and economic situations, the state of North-South relations, social and generational change, and the media.

Our statistical analyses suggest that overall favorable and unfavorable sentiment derives primarily from perceptions of the U.S.-South Korean bilateral relationship at any given time and the importance of U.S. forces to protecting South Korea's security. Using respondent-level data from past polling, we were able to explain, with a high degree of accuracy, individuals' favorable or unfavorable attitudes toward the U.S. by means of these two variables. A number of other individual-level characteristics and beliefs—what we called "lenses"—also modestly improved our predictions of favorable and unfavorable sentiment. Of these, the most important were age, educational attainment, and student status, each of which was found to be systematically associated with favorable or unfavorable sentiment. That is, younger and better-educated South Koreans typically tended to have the least favorable views of the U.S.

Both our qualitative historical analyses and our quantitative analyses of the available public opinion data suggest that South Koreans' assessments of the state of U.S.-South Korean relations are greatly influenced by the extent to which new developments appear to impinge on South Korean "sovereignty"; stoke South Koreans' sense of subservience, inequality, or unfairness; or can be successfully exploited by North Korea in its efforts to drive a wedge between the U.S. and South Korea.

Implications and Recommendations

The key implication of our work is that although we may have weathered the most recent downturn in U.S.-South Korean relations, and there are some reasons for hope that favorable sentiment toward the U.S. will increase, this is no time for complacency about South Koreans' views of the U.S. and the bilateral relationship.

Despite the efforts of U.S. and South Korean policymakers to put bilateral relations back on track, there has as yet been only a partial recovery in favorable sentiment toward the U.S. This seems to be attributable to the continued, widespread belief that the bilateral relationship is in poor shape, which appears to be placing drag on a full recovery. It cannot be known at this point whether a recovery in favorable sentiment has temporarily stalled, whether we are now at some sort of "tipping point," or whether attitudes have stabilized at a new, lower level. But the issue begs policy attention from both the U.S. and South Korea.

The challenge of dealing with North Korea (the Democratic People's Republic of Korea, or DPRK) will likely continue to test the alliance, as South Korea seeks to balance policies regarding inter-Korean affairs and the nuclear problem in the north, and as Pyongyang continues its efforts to create or exploit divisions between the U.S. and South Korea; there are many opportunities for miscalculation and missteps in the U.S.-ROK-DPRK *pas-de-trois* that could lead to friction in the alliance and to heightened ambivalence within the South Korean public.

Additionally, although many specific U.S. policies appear to be implicated in anti-American sentiment in South Korea, some unfavorable attitudes appear to transcend the current U.S. administration. Moreover—and somewhat ironically, given the U.S. government's encouragement—South Korean efforts to develop an "independent national defense" could have the undesirable effect of further eroding South Koreans' beliefs in the importance of U.S. forces to South Korea's security, a key foundation of overall favorable attitudes; the same line of reasoning would apply if the North Korean threat were to diminish or vanish.

As described in this report, younger cohorts have much less favorable attitudes than their parents, and better-educated South Koreans (and students) generally have less favorable attitudes than less well-educated ones. While the data cannot as yet be used to support an argument of demographic determinism—i.e., that simply through the normal replacement of the older generation of Koreans (who have generally more favorable attitudes) with new generations of better-educated Koreans (who have less favorable attitudes), we can expect further erosion in attitudes toward the U.S.—there are serious reasons for concern that such a shift could be taking place, and policymakers will need to monitor this question closely.

In consultation with our advisory group, we developed six recommendations for U.S. policymakers:

- First, the U.S. should explore opportunities for even more robust intelligence sharing, consultations, and other mechanisms that could help to harmonize U.S.-South Korean views on threats and appropriate responses. Our view is that the more both parties share a common picture of threats, the easier it will be to harmonize public statements and policies and avoid perceived divisions that might be exploited by North Korea.

- Second, the U.S. needs to do more now to persuade South Koreans that its interest in the region goes well beyond the North Korean threat and that it has a long-term interest in a peaceful, stable, and economically vital Northeast Asia. While the outcome of North Korea's efforts to preserve its regime and forestall a collapse cannot be foreseen with any clarity, it is important that South Koreans begin to consider the role of the U.S. in the region following either the collapse of the regime in Pyongyang or reunification.

- Third, the U.S. government should develop a public diplomacy strategy for South Korea that focuses on the legitimate grievances of those who criticize the U.S. (*pimi*), and does not attempt to change the views of those whose anti-Americanism (*panmi*) is ideological and more deeply rooted. The U.S. can, for example, highlight its support for South Korea's participation in the six-party talks on North Korea's nuclear capabilities, which could soften long-standing grievances that the U.S. does not take South Korean interests into account. To the maximum extent possible, the strategy should be a joint U.S.-South Korean one; the No Gun Ri commission, created to investigate an incident involving the deaths of South Koreans during the Korean War, might serve as a possible template.

- Fourth, the U.S. should work to better understand the extent to which (if at all) South Korea's educational system constitutes a structural source of anti-American sentiment. It would be useful for the U.S. and South Korea to jointly sponsor surveys and studies that (1) begin tracking the attitudes of South Korean youths age 13–18 on an annual basis and (2) analyze the contents of teaching curricula—including textbooks, syllabi and course notes, teaching methods used, teachers' incentives, and other factors that might be encouraging anti-American sentiment. Foundations also might sponsor these sorts of studies. The U.S. government also should (3) evaluate the potential contributions of educational exchange programs, including the Fulbright English Teaching Assistants (ETA) program.

- Fifth, the U.S. needs to better understand the role of the South Korean media in shaping attitudes toward the U.S. and should conduct or commission content analyses of South Korean media reporting on the U.S. and possibly of popular culture, such as music, television, and film.

- Our final recommendation is that the U.S. simply should not give up on Korea or Koreans: Their attitudes toward the U.S. are quite complex, and in spite of the recent downturn many measures have remained consistently and strongly positive. It remains very much in the U.S. interest to find ways to strengthen these attitudes while also seeking ways to avoid predictable friction that may arise as a result of perceived slights. And given South Koreans' increasing desire that their preferences and interests be fully considered on bilateral matters—especially dealings with North Korea—the U.S. will need to ensure a much higher level of bilateral coordination on policy matters if further rancor, and crystallization in unfavorable attitudes toward the U.S., are to be avoided.

As described in this report, South Koreans face a changing tableau of positive and negative images and messages about the U.S. and the U.S.-South Korean relationship—including the security alliance; trade, economic, and cultural relations; and other facets of the alliance—all filtered through the legacy of a complicated and at times tumultuous past and hopes for a better future. In the longer term, uncertainties about the prospects for continued economic growth, reunification, the future shape of Northeast Asia, and South Korea's need for U.S.

forces and the alliance introduce notes of both caution and stability in Koreans' attitudes toward the U.S. The result is a kaleidoscopic image or mosaic of the U.S. that harbors both gratitude and a desire to see a future South Korea that is a more independent and equal partner.

This basic ambivalence about the United States, which reflects South Koreans' efforts to balance their appreciation of the benefits that flow from a close relationship with the U.S. against continued aspirations arising from national pride and identity, imbues some South Korean attitudes toward the U.S. with a mercurial quality that can sometimes be breathtaking. But as described in this study, if the magnitude of the changes at times seems out of proportion to their proximate causes, the basic nature of the responses are frequently predictable and even avoidable. The challenge will be to ensure that South Koreans continue to have every reason to believe that the destinies of Koreans and Americans are intertwined and that this is, in the final analysis, a very good thing.

Acknowledgments

The authors with to thank a number of individuals who were quite helpful in the conduct of this study.

Our greatest debt of thanks is to our advisory group, all of whom took time from their busy schedules to provide advice to the study team: former U.S. Ambassador to South Korea Stephen W. Bosworth, Dean, Fletcher School of Law and Diplomacy, Tufts University; former U.S. Ambassador to South Korea Richard L. "Dixie" Walker, James F. Byrnes Ambassador-in-Residence, Walker Institute of International Studies, University of South Carolina; Victor Cha, Associate Professor, Department of Government and Edmund A. Walsh School of Foreign Service, Georgetown University; Dr. James Marshall, Office of Research, U.S. Department of State; Robert Scalapino, Robson Research Professor of Government Emeritus, Institute of East Asian Studies, University of California, Berkeley; Doh C. Shin, Professor of Political Science, University of Missouri, Columbia; and Gi Wook Shin, Associate Professor of Sociology and Senior Fellow at the Institute for International Studies, Stanford University. We also thank former U.S. Ambassador Jack Pritchard; William Watts, President of Potomac Associates; and RAND colleague Julie DaVanzo for their careful technical reviews.

Within the RAND Corporation, we wish to thank Nina Hachigian, Director of the RAND Center for Asia Pacific Policy (CAPP); Bruce Bennett; Jennifer Kavanaugh; Somi Seong; Greg Treverton; Rachel Swanger; Patricia Clark; Nurith Bernstein; Claudia McCowan; RAND's reference librarians: Amy Atchison, Kristin McCool, Barbara Neff, Roberta Shanman; and Laurie Rennie.

Outside of RAND, we would like to thank Allan Song of the Smith Richardson Foundation; Larry Diamond of the Hoover Institution, Stanford University; Young-Sup Han, Korea National Defense University; Meril James, Secretary General, Gallup International; General Dong-Shin Kim, former Minister of National Defense, Republic of Korea; Spencer H. Kim, President, Pacific Century Institute; Former Ambassador Lee In-ho, President, The Korea Foundation; Shin-Bom Lee, a member of South Korea's National Assembly; Derek Mitchell and Kazuyo Kato, both of the Center for Strategic and International Studies (CSIS); Nicole Speulda of the Pew Research Center for People and the Press; and JinSoo Yang of Gallup Korea.

This report is dedicated to one of the members of our advisory group, Richard L. "Dixie" Walker, who passed away in the summer of 2003. We will greatly miss him and are saddened that we cannot have the opportunity to thank him for his wise counsel.

Acronyms

APEC   Asia-Pacific Economic Cooperation

CSIS   Center for Strategic and International Studies

DPRK   Democratic Peoples Republic of Korea

FBIS   Foreign Broadcast Information Service

FSX   Jet fighter plane

GNP   Grand National Party

IAEA   International Atomic Energy Agency

KEDO   Korean Peninsula Energy Development Organization

KEPCO   South Korean power company

KINU   Korea Institute of National Unification

LWR   Light Water Reactor

MAC   Military Armistice Commission

MDP   Millennium Democratic Party

NGO   Non-Governmental Organization

NNSC   Neutral Nations Supervisory Commission

NPT   Nuclear Proliferation Treaty

ROK   Republic of Korea

SOFA   Status of Forces Agreement

USFK   United States Forces Korea

1. Introduction

An increase in expressions of anti-American sentiment among South Koreans in the spring and summer of 2002 led to heightened concern among many South Korean observers that one of the pillars of the U.S.-South Korean alliance—a strong belief among the South Korean people in the continued importance of the U.S.-ROK alliance, and an equally strong commitment to its continuation—might be in jeopardy.

The spectacle of candlelight vigils, demonstrations, and burnings of American flags in late 2002 and early 2003, the most obvious and visible manifestations of recent anti-American sentiment among South Koreans, raised questions in many circles about the durability of support for the U.S. military presence and bilateral alliance with South Korea. Less well understood, however, was whether these surface currents accurately reflected most South Koreans' views toward the U.S., how the most recent period compared with the past, and what larger forces have tended to animate attitudes toward the U.S.[1]

It has long been the U.S. position that it will continue to maintain U.S. forces in Korea as long as that is the desire of South Koreans themselves. For U.S. policymakers then, the key question is whether South Koreans support the continuation of the U.S. military presence and the alliance. Thus, understanding the relative prevalence and trends in various strains of anti-U.S. feeling lies at the heart of understanding the nature of the challenge that U.S. and South Korean leaders might face in sustaining support for the alliance.

Some South Korean observers have usefully divided the concept of anti-Americanism (*panmi*) into several distinct strains:

- anti-Americanism (*panmijuui*), a deeply rooted conviction held primarily by radical student organizations and leftist scholars and journalists, which actively excludes and aggressively opposes the United States and its policies

- pragmatic anti-Americanism, represented by moderate nongovernmental organizations (NGOs) that focus on such specific issues as the Status of

---

[1]Anti-Americanism in Korea has been the subject of numerous studies over the years, including Shorrock (1986); Kim (1989); Clark (1991); Lee (1993); Shin (1995); Shin (1996); and Risse (2001). For an excellent historical review of Koreans' views on the U.S., see Kyong-Dong (1993).

Forces Agreement (SOFA), environmental damage, wartime operational control of South Korean forces, rather than denying the U.S. itself

- anti-American sentiment (*panmijongso*), a passive, more widely held view that results in dissatisfaction about, or criticism of, some aspects of the U.S. or U.S. policy and tends to respond in a somewhat episodic and emotional manner to salient developments.[2]

Mindful of the possibility of different strains of unfavorable sentiment toward the U.S., we sought in this study to address gaps in understanding South Korean attitudes in the current period by addressing, principally through an analysis of the available public opinion data, three key research questions:

(1) What are the trends in South Koreans' attitudes toward the United States and is the conventional wisdom that they recently have deteriorated correct?

(2) What are the sources of South Korean attitudes toward the U.S., and what are their trends over time?

(3) What are the implications of these trends for U.S. policy toward Korea and larger security interests?

As suggested by the research questions, the focus of this study was on the South Korean *mass public's* attitudes toward the U.S., and not on the attitudes, preferences, or actions taken by South Korean political leaders to ensure a healthy alliance and smooth working relationship with the U.S. This is an important distinction.

The focus of this study on favorable and unfavorable sentiment toward the U.S. within the South Korean mass public does not in any way challenge the proposition that most South Korean political and military leaders—as stewards of a now 50-year alliance with the U.S.—remain committed to a healthy and strong bilateral relationship with the U.S. The extent to which ordinary South Koreans may be less committed, however, is of obvious policy interest both the U.S. and to them as well, because democratic theory—and historical experience—suggest that leadership often is needed to build and sustain support for contentious policies, and that public support is needed to sustain policies over the long run.

Finally, although this report does not address the decline in favorable sentiment toward the U.S. that reportedly has occurred in many other countries around the world, it is important to note that some events, such as the U.S. war in Iraq,

---

[2]See Kim (October 21, 2002), and Kim (October 22, 2002). See also Clark (1991), especially pp. 148–150.

appear to have affected other publics in much the same way they affected South Koreans.[3]

Approach

This study relied upon two complementary analytic approaches.

First, we undertook an historical review of U.S.-South Korean relations to place the present period in the context of its larger historical legacy, to identify past sources of friction in the relationship, and to generate alternative hypotheses that could be explored through public opinion data. This effort included an analysis of developments during two recent, critical periods—the North Korean nuclear crisis and its aftermath, from 1992 to 1996, and the Kim Dae Jung "Sunshine Policy" and its aftermath, from 1998 to the present.

Second, we collected public opinion data that bore on the question of South Korean attitudes toward the U.S., the alliance, reunification, the threat from the north, and other related issues.

It is important to note that the analysis of public opinion data is exceedingly detailed, tedious work. One needs, of course, to attend to the population sampled and the sample size, but such matters as the timing of the poll, the specific structure and wording of the questions, question order, "house effects," and other, often difficult-to-quantify factors can be equally important . Given that question wording and structure and other factors can have such dramatic effects on outcomes, we consistently sought in our study to emphasize those results that appeared to be robust, i.e., those that had a reasonably substantial weight of evidence, and that were representative of a larger body of public opinion.[4] We also reported individual questions in cases where we felt that these provided perspective that otherwise would be lacking. At the end of the day, though, studies such as ours rely heavily upon "found objects"—questions that were asked by others, often for very different purposes, which can contain all sorts of idiosyncrasies.

To address our research question about changes in South Korean attitudes over time, we relied upon trend data, i.e., identically worded questions asked of the same population over time, by the same polling organization. For our trend

---

[3]See the results of the Pew Research Center for People and the Press' Global Attitudes project, which are available at http://people-press.org/reports/.

[4]For an excellent review of the factors that can account for differences in public opinion results, and a strong argument in favor of a "weight of evidence" approach, see Kagay (1992).

data, we relied primarily on polling by Gallup Korea for the Office of Research in the U.S. Department of State from 1988 to 2001. These polls used face-to-face interviews to ask approximately 1,600 South Korean respondents a standard battery of questions about the U.S., the bilateral relationship, perceived threats, and other matters of interest. Because of the strict comparability of these questions over time, their relatively large sample size (which typically gives results a margin of error of plus or minus three percentage points at the 95-percent confidence interval), continuity in the polling organization and its sampling frame, the relatively high response rate, and other features, these data provided the best available basis for reliably assessing trends over time.

We also used polling from other sources such as Gallup Korea, *JoongAng Ilbo*, and other South Korean sources, where it was possible to construct true trends from these data that might cross-validate the State Department data. And to provide a more current snapshot of attitudes, RAND collaborated with the Center for Strategic and International Studies (CSIS) and the *JoongAng Ilbo* newspaper by constructing a list of questions for two polls of South Koreans' attitudes toward the U.S. that were conducted in September 2003, on the 50th anniversary of the U.S.-ROK alliance, and analyzing the results of these polls.[5]

To assess various hypotheses about the potential sources of attitudes toward the U.S., we relied upon marginals (the overall or subgroup percentages responding to various question options), and cross-tabulations from public opinion polling that came from a wide variety of sources. These included the Office of Research in the U.S. Department of State; Gallup Korea and Gallup International; the Korea Press Foundation's KINDS database of news reporting; the Foreign Broadcast Information Service (FBIS); the Korean Institute for National Unification (KINU); The Pew Research Center for People and the Press; The Harris Poll; and the Korea Barometer Survey.

We also used data from several respondent-level datasets from polling done by the U.S. Department of State in South Korea in the early 1990s that were archived with the National Archives and Records Administration and The Roper Center for Public Opinion Research.[6] Using these data, we were able to statistically model the considerations that are associated with favorable or unfavorable attitudes toward the U.S., and predict, with a fairly high degree of accuracy, overall sentiment using a small number of sensible, policy-relevant variables.

---

[5]See Larson (2004).

[6]The characteristics of the datasets that we used and the results of our respondent-level statistical modeling are reported in a separate working paper (Savych and Larson, forthcoming) that will be available for download from RAND's website.

It is important to note that the quality and utility of the data from the hundreds of other polls we compiled varied greatly.[7] Whereas South Korean polling organizations generally report polling dates, the population of interest, the sample size, and (usually) the margin of error, they have a propensity to change question structure and wording from poll to poll, which reduces their comparability, and they generally fail to provide detailed information about response rates and other technical features that also are of some interest. Our approach was to use these other sources to help fill in knowledge gaps—for example, about differences between various subgroups of interest—or to cross-validate findings from other surveys, but to generally try to avoid basing findings on a single polling result.

Taken together—the interdisciplinary approach, the range of issues considered, and the mixture of trend, bivariate, and multivariate analyses—we believe that our study is the first of its kind. Our approach has provided a comprehensive and empirically-based analysis of the factors that go into South Koreans' attitudes toward the U.S., and it considers a wider range of data sources, a larger number of polling results, and a more appropriate combination of aggregate- and individual-level analyses than has been done before.

Organization of This Report

This report is organized as follows:

- Chapter 2 provides a qualitative historical analysis of U.S.-South Korean relations, identifies the factors that most recently appear to have created frictions that have influenced Koreans' attitudes toward the U.S., and provides a number of hypotheses about the sources of South Koreans' attitudes toward the U.S. that could be explored through the public opinion data.

- Chapter 3 addresses, through trend analyses of the available data on the matter, the question of whether there has been a recent downturn in South Koreans' attitudes toward the U.S.

- Chapter 4 builds upon the historical analysis in Chapter Two and the trend analyses in Chapter Three by exploring the relationships between favorable attitudes toward the U.S. and a variety of individual- and societal-level factors that serve as sources of attitudes toward the U.S.

---

[7]The results of our data collection efforts are reported in a separate working paper (Baik and Larson, forthcoming) that will be available for download from RAND's website. In most cases, we were able to report the dates, sample size, type of interview, and margin of error. Only rarely were response rates and other technical information reported, however.

- Chapter 5 presents the implications of our analyses, and recommendations to U.S. government policymakers.

2. The Past as Prologue

This chapter examines the historical context for South Korean attitudes toward the United States. The chapter first reviews the major events in Korea's modern history that helped shape these attitudes. This is designed to highlight the complexity of the historical legacy and identify potential "hot button" issues emerging from Korea's modern experience that, when excited, influence Korean views of the U.S. today.   It then examines two key periods over the last decade during which the U.S.-ROK relationship was a subject of intense discussions in South Korea and Korean views of the U.S. fluctuated significantly. This part of the chapter reviews the major developments in each period and describes their impact on South Korean attitudes. The chapter concludes with an assessment of the role such developments played as influences on South Korean attitudes toward the United States.

Korea's Historic Experience

In this 50th anniversary year of the U.S.-ROK security alliance, there has understandably been much official toasting of the alliance's strength and longevity. For over five decades the U.S.-ROK relationship has helped maintain peace and foster prosperity not only in South Korea but also throughout East Asia, while it has advanced a wide range of other important U.S. and South Korean interests.[1] Viewed from a Korean perspective, however, Korea's experience with the U.S. over the past century presents a more mixed picture.

Although the U.S. established formal diplomatic relations with Korea (the "Hermit Kingdom") in 1882, bilateral contacts were minimal over the next two decades. The roots of U.S. involvement in Korea's fortunes date more directly to Russia's defeat in the Russo-Japanese War (1904–1905) and Japan's emergence as the dominant foreign power in Korea. As Japan extended its control over the peninsula, Korean representatives appealed to the U.S. to protect Korea's independence. President Theodore Roosevelt considered this request but, seeing no way to prevent Japanese domination of Korea and being personally

---

[1] For a more detailed account of the historical background and mutual benefits, from which parts of this review are drawn, see Levin (forthcoming).

contemptuous of Koreans, he rejected it.[2] Instead, Roosevelt authorized his Secretary of State to sign a secret agreement with Japan in July 1905 (the Taft-Katsura Agreement) that recognized Japan's prerogatives in Korea in exchange for American freedom of action in the Philippines. The U.S. also served as sponsor and mid-wife to the Treaty of Portsmouth, a few months later which involved, among other things, Russia's formal acknowledgment of Japan's paramount interests in Korea. For many Koreans, U.S. acquiescence in, if not active facilitation of, Japan's subjugation of Korea, which lasted until Japan's surrender in World War II forty years later, is an enduring stain on America's image.

This less-than-auspicious beginning was partially improved at the Cairo Conference in December 1943 when the U.S. publicly pledged that "in due course Korea shall become free and independent."[3] Most South Koreans were jubilant, interpreting "in due course" to mean "soon" or "shortly." But no U.S. or other allied leader had any idea at the time how Korean self-rule could actually be accomplished, and U.S. policy was predicated on a belief in the gradual introduction of self-rule into colonial areas lacking experience in self-government.[4] Accordingly, for the remainder of World War II they neglected any detailed planning for Korea's post-war future, assuming that it would be placed under some form of international trusteeship. When the Yalta Conference did not even mention Korea, many Korean leaders suspected that Korea had been sacrificed to secure Soviet involvement in the war against Japan. Some saw U.S. actions as close to a betrayal.

Faced with the sudden surrender of Japan in 1945, the U.S. made three fateful decisions. The first was to divide the Korean peninsula along the 38th parallel, a "convenient administrative dividing line" to facilitate arrangements for processing the surrender and repatriation of Japanese troops in Korea.[5] Since Soviet troops had already moved south of the 38th parallel, this decision reflected realities on the ground rather than some purely arbitrary U.S. action. But in a land with hundreds of years of history as a single, unified country, it was highly controversial from the beginning. Koreans on both left and right sides of the

---

[2] On Roosevelt's attitudes, see Nahm (1982). For a detailed analysis of the period, see Conroy (1960), p. 329. For standard Korean and American histories, see Han (1974), especially pp. 447–448, and Fairbank, Reischauer, and Craig (1965), pp. 479–483 respectively.

[3] The complete text of the statement, agreed to by the U.S., China, and Great Britain, said that the "three great powers, mindful of the enslavement of the people of Korea, are determined that in due course Korea shall become free and independent." Borton (1970), p. 445.

[4] Allen, *Korea's Syngman Rhee* (1960), pp. 65–66.

[5] Acheson (1970), p. 581.

political spectrum expressed strong dissatisfaction with the country's division, even on a temporary basis.

The second decision was to govern the southern part of the country through direct U.S. military rule. Koreans, as noted above, had almost universally looked forward to Japan's defeat as bringing about their "liberation." They responded to Japan's surrender with frenetic political activity.[6] An interim government was even formed which governed the country in the weeks between Japan's surrender and the arrival of U.S. military authorities. The decision of U.S. military authorities to place the country under U.S. military occupation set off large demonstrations against the military government. When the U.S. decided that, notwithstanding the strong Korean aspiration for independence, it had no choice but to continue with wartime allied agreements and proposed an international trusteeship over Korea at the Moscow conference in December 1945 (which the Soviets accepted), massive demonstrations erupted throughout the country. The subsequent acceptance of trusteeship by Korea's communist groups, under direct orders from Moscow, diluted the political effect of this decision but it did little to improve the tarnished U.S. image.

The third decision, taken three years later, was to terminate the U.S. military occupation because of pressing needs elsewhere and to support the establishment of a separate, independent state in the south (since Moscow prevented free elections throughout the country). Unlike the decision on trusteeship, which South Koreans almost universally reviled, reactions to the decision to hold separate elections in the south and create an independent South Korean state were sharply divided. Conservatives and moderate nationalists, who had long called for the establishment of a free, capitalist, independent state, supported the decision and sought an active role for the U.S. in strengthening and supporting the nascent nation. Progressives and more radical nationalists, who believed that separate elections would formalize the division of Korea, strongly opposed the decision and sought instead the withdrawal of U.S. military forces as a means for facilitating peaceful unification. This intense ideological split recast in different but aggravated form the sharp schism that had rent the Korean independence movement throughout the first half of the 20th century.[7] It also made the U.S. role in Korea a focus of sharp political and ideological

---

[6] Detailed accounts of the tumultuous period in Korea may be found in Henderson (1968),. Oliver (1978), and Cummings (1990).

[7] For more details, see Levin and Han (2002), pp. 54–58.

confrontation, a confrontation over issues pertaining to very origin of the South Korean state.[8]

The Korean War and decades of strong authoritarian rule by South Korean governments largely silenced debate over the U.S. role in Korea, but they neither resolved the basic issues of contention nor removed the political and emotional residue from the previous U.S. actions. In particular, they did nothing to resolve the underlying ideological divide in South Korea between conservatives and progressives and the competing nationalisms that affect most major issues pertaining to the United States. As a result, the U.S. role became a focus of contention every time political controls were loosened in South Korea.[9] Perceived U.S. political support for successive authoritarian governments reinforced this public contention. While such perceptions were at best incomplete characterizations of U.S. policy, they were widely shared in South Korea. For a minority, they fueled strong anti-American sentiment.

U.S. actions during the Kwangju crisis in May 1980, when popular unrest following the assassination of then-President Park Chung-Hee led to a brutal South Korean military crackdown, were doubly consequential in this respect. They infuriated most South Koreans on the left side of the political spectrum who, inaccurately but fervently, insisted that American leaders actively supported the bloody crackdown and broader repression of democracy in Korea. And they agitated the South Korean military and others on the right side of the spectrum, who saw steps taken by the U.S. to censure the ROK government as being insensitive to the "realities" of Korea's situation and inconsistent with U.S. security commitments.[10] One effect was to make the U.S. the lightening rod for widespread public unhappiness with the Chun Doo-Hwan regime, which seized power shortly after Park's assassination. Another was to fuel doubts—which had been acutely stimulated a few years earlier by former President Jimmy Carter's aborted plan to withdraw U.S. combat troops from Korea—about the reliability of the United States as a strategic partner.

Such developments represent the downside of Korea's historical experience with the U.S. But there is also an obvious upside. The U.S. ended Japan's four-and-a-half decade colonial rule over Korea and engineered the establishment of a free,

---

[8]One of the members of our advisory group, Professor Robert A. Scalapino of the University of California, Berkeley, noted that Secretary of State Dean Acheson's failure to include South Korea as a country that lay within the U.S.' defense perimeter in his statement on the matter some months before the outbreak of the Korean War may have contributed to Kim Il Sung's belief that the U.S. would not intervene in the event of a North Korean effort to unify the peninsula by force.

[9] For the classic account, see Han (1974).

[10] Wickham (2000), pp. 176–177.

independent South Korean state. The U.S. preserved South Korea's independence when North Korea launched a massive invasion in 1950, ultimately suffering some 30,000 U.S. dead among a total of nearly 137,000 casualties. And the U.S. ensured South Korea's continuing security through a formal defense commitment—which includes the provision of a nuclear umbrella over the ROK—and a close bilateral alliance which involves a combined defense posture and the sustained stationing of tens of thousands of U.S. troops in South Korea. Frequent South Korean characterizations of this alliance as one "forged in blood" thus has real meaning in a Korean context. So too does President Roh's recent praise of U.S. forces for having "inherited the great legacy of those who came before them and who protected freedom and democracy with their sweat and blood."[11]

As part of its efforts to strengthen the bilateral alliance, moreover, the U.S. actively supported the development and improvement of South Korea's armed forces, serving as the source for almost 80 percent of the ROK's military purchases and most of its technical training and advanced weapons. The U.S. also provided South Korea an enormous amount of military and economic assistance. Between 1950 and 1988, for example, the U.S. gave South Korea over $5.5 billion in free military assistance, in addition to nearly $9 billion of other military aid.[12] U.S. economic assistance totaled some $3.8 billion between the ending of Japanese rule in 1945 and the onset of South Korea's rapid economic growth in the beginning of the 1970s alone.[13] The U.S. also provided strong political support to facilitate the ROK's normalization of relations with the major powers, as well as its integration into world political and economic institutions.

The general result is a complex mixture of feelings among South Koreans about the United States. On one side there is gratitude, fondness, and respect—both for the values and ideals the U.S. represents and for the extensive support the U.S. has provided South Korea over the last five decades. On the other side there is a lingering sense of resentment and distrust—both for the continuing U.S. influence over South Korean fortunes and for past U.S. actions that many Koreans feel have not taken into account Korean interests. The complexity of these feelings are heightened by the tension between the widespread South Korean appreciation of the benefits Korea receives from the U.S.-ROK alliance and the annoyance many Koreans feel at their continuing dependence on the United States.

---

[11] This quote comes from Roh's speech marking the 55th anniversary of Armed Forces Day on October 1, 2003 and is available online at the ROK Blue House web site, http://www.cwd.go.kr.

[12] ROK Ministry of National Defense (2002), p. 40.

[13] Niksch (2002).

For these reasons, the kind of continuing impact history has on Korean attitudes toward Japan—a strong and nearly universal feeling somewhere between dislike and antipathy—finds no complete analogue in the case of the United States. Korean attitudes toward the U.S. are both more complex and less visceral. Still, Korea's experience with the U.S. has left some historical residue. One trace is the lingering suspicions that South Koreans perennially have about U.S. intentions. Hardly a single high-level U.S.-ROK meeting takes place without some form of U.S. "reassurance" about its plans and/or commitments. But the most important trace is the strong sensitivity South Koreans show toward policies or actions perceived as affecting their ability to control their own destiny. Such actions are often perceived as threats to Korea's sovereignty, even when they might appear to outsiders to lack either this intent or quality. Indeed, this sensitivity is so strong that it suggests at least one "hot button" issue emerging from Korea's historical experience: almost anything that suggests the subordination of Korean interests to those of outside powers.

Transition to the 1990s

The years Roh Tae-Woo served as South Korea's president (1988–1992) represent an important transition period, with a number of truly historic developments. One was South Korea's breakthrough in establishing normal relations with its powerful communist neighbors and larger international community. This breakthrough, a result of changes in the communist world and Roh's own policy of "Nordpolitik," saw South Korea normalize relations with the Soviet Union in 1990, gain admission (along with North Korea) into the United Nations in 1991, and establish diplomatic relations with China in 1992. Nordpolitik broadened South Korea's diplomatic playing field while reducing the likelihood of outside support for potential North Korean aggression.

South Korea also began a serious pursuit of peaceful coexistence with North Korea during this period. This pursuit involved an effort to expand exchanges, trade, and other economic cooperation with the North as steps toward creating a "joint national community" in which both Koreas could prosper. The crowning achievement of this effort was the February 1992 "Agreement on Reconciliation, Non-Aggression, and Exchanges and Cooperation between the South and the North" (commonly referred to as the "Basic Agreement"). This landmark agreement committed the two sides to respect each other's political systems, never use force or threaten military action, and actively promote inter-Korean trade, travel, and cooperation. It also heralded the long-term possibility of unification on South Korean terms through a gradual process of peaceful coexistence.

The really big development in this period, however, was the collapse of the Soviet Union in 1991. The impact of this historic event on Korea is not widely appreciated. This is not entirely surprising. The demise of the USSR not only failed to precipitate the collapse of North Korea (as it did the Communist states of Eastern Europe), it didn't even replace the tenuous armistice arrangements in Korea with a durable peace agreement. But the USSR's collapse nonetheless had a profound impact beneath the surface by further isolating Pyongyang and dramatically accelerating the shift in the inter-Korean balance of power in Seoul's favor.[14] The consequences were particularly acute for North Korea. Deprived of Soviet support, Pyongyang stepped up its effort to acquire weapons of mass destruction to compensate for its declining conventional capability. The loss of Soviet assistance also precipitated a decade-long free-fall in the North Korean economy.

The collapse of the Soviet Union, however, also had significant consequences in South Korea. South Korean pride and self-confidence soared, as the already substantial economic gap with North Korea widened dramatically and annual South Korean military spending far outpaced what Pyongyang could afford. Public views of the North also began to change, particularly after the height of the nuclear crisis in 1993–1994. Instead of a menacing North Korea on the verge of sudden attack, South Koreans began to see a hapless North Korea on the verge of implosion. One effect was to increase South Korea's perceived stake in North Korea's evolution. Another was to spawn a public tendency to regard Pyongyang more as a life-style threat—in the sense of South Korea being overwhelmed by refugees or having to bear the astronomical costs of unification—than as an imminent security danger. As the view spread by the late 1990s that North Korea was simply unable to initiate a large-scale conventional conflict, South Korean threat perceptions declined sharply, with public feelings toward the North shifting from "fear" to something between "sympathy" and "pity."[15] The perceived importance of the U.S. security guarantee declined in the process.

A final historic development was the beginning of democratization in South Korea. While still fledgling in this period, Roh Tae-Woo's government allowed a significant loosening of domestic political constraints. One effect was to remove security and unification issues from the exclusive purview of specialists and open up public discussions. Another was to reactivate the ideological fault line that plagued Korea throughout the 20th century but especially since the end of

---

[14]Armacost (2001).

[15] For a useful account, see Omestad (2003).

World War II. More broadly, democratization brought with it political changes that involved a perceptible shift in the ideological center of gravity. Recent polls confirm a decided move by Koreans to the left over time, with opinion leaders being decidedly more "progressive" (i.e., liberal) than other citizens surveyed.[16] Democratization also spawned the growth of a large and vibrant civil society which, oppressed for decades under successive South Korean governments, is distrustful of authority and generally not as well disposed toward the U.S. as other parts of Korean society such as the older generation of Koreans.

These historic developments set the stage for two critical periods in the last decade that saw significant movement in South Korean attitudes toward the United States. These were the period of the U.S.-DPRK nuclear crisis and its aftermath (1992–1996) and that of the inter-Korean summit and its aftermath (2000–2002).

The Nuclear Crisis (1992–1996)

A common view of the nuclear crisis is that it began with North Korea's announcement of its intent to withdraw from the Nuclear Non-Proliferation Treaty (NPT) in March 1993. It then ratcheted up through stages until former U.S. President Jimmy Carter went to Pyongyang in July 1994 and secured a pledge from Kim Il Sung to freeze North Korea's nuclear program and pursue high level talks with the United States about dismantling the North's nuclear facilities. The crisis ended a few months later (October 1994) when U.S.-DPRK negotiations produced the so-called "Agreed Framework," which froze North Korea's overt nuclear program and allowed international inspections of its existing nuclear plants in exchange for two light water reactors and 500,000 tons of heavy fuel oil annually.[17] While this common view is not far off the mark as it pertains to the crisis between the U.S. and North Korea it is inaccurate as it pertains to U.S.-South Korean relations. In the latter case, the seeds of the crisis were planted considerably sooner and they stayed in bloom much longer.

The point of departure was the beginning of 1992 and the formal entry into force of two historic agreements between the two Koreas. The first was the "Basic

---

[16] *JoongAng Ilbo*, February 11, 2003.

[17] For a detailed, if highly critical, account of U.S. policy on the North Korean nuclear issue, see Sigal (1998). The text of the Agreed Framework, formally titled "Agreed Framework Between the United States of America and the Democratic People's Republic of Korea," is included in the appendix of this volume, along with the texts of other important U.S.-DPRK agreements. The Agreed Framework is also available online at http://www.kedo.org. For a useful summary of the key aspects, see the fact sheet put out by the Arms Control Association entitled "The U.S.-North Korean Agreed Framework at a Glance," available at http://www.armscontrol.org.

Agreement" alluded to above. This landmark agreement committed the two sides to respect each other's political systems, work together to transform the state of armistice into a state of peace, and take mutual steps to realize arms reductions, including the elimination of weapons of mass destruction. The second, which took effect the same day, was the "Joint Declaration of the Denuclearization of the Korean Peninsula," or "Joint Declaration" for short. In this agreement, both sides pledged not to "test, manufacture, produce, receive, possess, store, deploy or use nuclear weapons" or "possess nuclear reprocessing and uranium enrichment facilities," while they agreed to conduct mutual inspections of the other side's facilities in order to verify its denuclearization.[18] Both agreements set up elaborate institutional machinery, including a Joint Military Commission and Joint Nuclear Control Commission, to implement their terms and respective commitments.

To be sure, questions were raised almost from the beginning about the significance of these agreements. Two developments were particularly important. One was evidence discovered by the International Atomic Energy Agency (IAEA) in the summer of 1992, a few months after North Korea concluded a safeguards agreement with the IAEA, that it had reprocessed an unknown amount of spent fuel on three separate occasions. This evidence, which was at odds with Pyongyang's official report to the IAEA about its nuclear program and assurances to South Korea, raised serious questions about both the North's nuclear intentions and capabilities and precipitated IAEA demands—backed by the U.S.—for "special inspections" of the North's facilities.

The second development had to do with North Korea's behavior in the various joint North-South committees established pursuant to the two agreements. While some committees made modest progress, Pyongyang used others primarily to try to advance long-standing political objectives, many of which appeared designed to stimulate unrest in South Korea and/or drive a wedge between the ROK and the United States.[19] Progress was minimal on the nuclear issue in particular. Although the Joint Nuclear Control Commission met more than twenty times over the course of 1992, North Korea resisted progress not only on mutual North-South nuclear inspections but also on the rules or guidelines for such cross inspections. Eventually, the self-set deadline for adoption of inspection procedures passed unmet.

---

[18] The texts of both agreements are in ROK Ministry of National Unification (1996), pp. 200–209.

[19] In the Political Affairs Subcommittee, for example, the North pressed for such things as abolishing or revising treaties each of them had signed with other countries and pledging not to cooperate "in the acts of any third country that might infringe on the interests of either side." Ibid., pp. 96–102.

Still, these agreements were critical in at least two respects. They formally committed North Korea in a North-South negotiating context to forgo the development of nuclear or other weapons of mass destruction, reinforcing the DPRK's international obligations as a signatory of the nuclear Non-Proliferation Treaty (NPT). And they established direct North-South channels as the agreed-upon means for pursuing tension reduction between the two Koreas and resolving potential issues of contention. Both of these objectives were at the top of South Korea's policy agenda.

Unfortunately, both of these objectives were also challenged by North Korea's March 1993 announcement of its intent to withdraw from the NPT when the IAEA pressed for special inspections. In making the surprise announcement, North Korea clearly sought to create a sense of crisis. This was designed to increase North Korean bargaining leverage and gain greater control over the agenda for negotiations by, in part, shifting the focus from North Korea's actions to those of the U.S. and IAEA.[20] It also was designed to deflect attention away from the North's *past* nuclear activities toward concessions it might receive in exchange for constraints on its *future* program, while establishing a direct relationship with the U.S. without having to deal with South Korea.[21] These North Korean goals were all unacceptable to South Korea, of course. Three days after the North Korean announcement the ROK government suspended all inter-Korean talks and economic exchanges.

To the U.S., on the other hand, North Korean actions not only raised tensions on the Korean peninsula and threatened a potentially disastrous military conflict. They also called into question the survivability of the global non-proliferation regime—an important U.S. strategic interest. The new Clinton administration accordingly decided to initiate discussions with North Korea in an effort to seek a political resolution of the crisis, and the first round of U.S.-North Korean talks were held in June 1993. This decision generated considerable concern in South Korea about U.S. intentions. It also stimulated intense resentment at South Korea's exclusion from a process that directly affected critical South Korean interests but over which the ROK had little influence.[22] On July 1, Kim Young Sam harshly criticized the negotiations in interviews with foreign media.

---

[20] North Korea's announcement stated that its withdrawal would never be reversed "until the U.S. nuclear threat is abandoned and the IAEA recovers its independence and objectivity." *Rodong Sinmun*, March 12, 1993.

[21] Snyder (1999), pp. 69–70.

[22] Among other things, the U.S.-DPRK talks served to "remind South Korean officials of their own sense of helplessness at being sidelined from an issue that directly impinged on South Korean national interests but was beyond the control of the leadership in Seoul." Ibid., p. 108.

Over the second half of 1993 the two newly elected presidents, President Clinton and President Kim Young Sam, held two separate summit meetings (in July and November) to address South Korean sensitivities about U.S. dealings with North Korea and coordinate their respective approaches. At the November summit the two leaders appeared to bridge the gap between them by agreeing to discuss with North Korea a "thorough and broad" approach to the issues that divide the three countries with a view to resolving the nuclear issue "once and for all."[23] Reflecting South Korea's great unhappiness at its exclusion from these discussions, however, they insisted that the North begin a dialogue with South Korea as one of the conditions for the resumption of negotiations (the other condition being to ensure the continuity of IAEA safeguards).

Despite the November summit agreement, South Korean sensitivities, and simmering resentment at the ROK's exclusion from the negotiating process, remained strong. This was clear from a hard-line speech President Kim gave to the South Korean National Assembly reporting on the outcome of his second summit meeting. "In our meeting," President Kim said, "President Clinton and I clearly defined how the United States and Korea would deal with the issue of North Korea's nuclear development. President Clinton and I reconfirmed that *IAEA inspections of North Korea's nuclear facilities, mutual South-North nuclear inspections and continued intra-Korean dialogue are prerequisites to resolving the issue* [emphasis added]."[24] Continuing in a way that suggests that the real intended audience was the U.S. rather than the National Assembly, Kim added:

> . . . We made it crystal clear that a guarantee by North Korea of the transparency of its nuclear policy, on which the very existence of our 70 million compatriots depends, can never be subject to negotiation. Assuming that North Korea finally does so we will try to negotiate complete and comprehensive measures to settle the nuclear issue fundamentally. We confirmed, however, that *the Korean government will have the final say on issues affecting the peninsula*, including the Team Spirit military exercise. *This means the Koreanization of issues pertaining to the Korean Peninsula* [emphases added].[25]

---

[23] "Text of Presidents Kim Young-Sam and Bill Clinton at the Joint Press Conference, *Korea Annual 1994*, pp. 352–353.

[24] "President Kim Young-Sam's Speech to the National Assembly on the APEC Leaders Meeting and His Visit to the United States," ibid., pp. 348–350.

[25] Ibid., p. 349. Scott Snyder suggests that Kim Young Sam had received word of preliminary, internal U.S. deliberations on possible responses to North Korean proposals for a "package solution" to the nuclear issue, which South Korea had not been briefed on. This heightened South Korean suspicions "that the United States might try to cut a secret deal with North Korea" and underscored "the fact up to that point, South Korea had been kept on the sidelines of the negotiating process." See Snyder (1999), p. 110.

The U.S. continued talks with North Korea over the next several months in an effort to find a way to both move U.S.-DPRK negotiations forward and accommodate the key South Korean "prerequisites." In February 1994 the two sides reached agreement on a four-point plan called the "Agreed Conclusion."[26] The plan did not mention anything about "mutual North-South inspections," as both Koreas had agreed upon in their February 1992 agreements and as South Korea had insisted upon thereafter. But it did include North Korean pledges to resume bilateral talks with South Korea on exchanging high-level envoys to restart North-South dialogue and permit IAEA inspections of North Korea's nuclear facilities.

Meanwhile, South Korea continued its efforts to get itself into the game and gain greater control over U.S. dealings with North Korea. On February 25 for example, the day the Agreed Conclusion was reached, Kim Young Sam announced that he would seek a North-South summit meeting as the means for resolving the nuclear dispute. And on February 27, the ROK government announced that it would resume the suspended U.S.-ROK Team Spirit military exercises—even though the first point of the four-point Agreed Conclusion committed the U.S. to suspend these joint military exercises—unless IAEA inspections and a North-South special envoy exchange took place.

Any sense of forward movement came to a halt on March 19 when North Korea's chief delegate at a North-South meeting called to discuss the exchange of special envoys threatened that Seoul would be turned into a "sea of fire" if war were to break out on the peninsula. This set off an intense public reaction in South Korea and a downward spiral in both U.S. and ROK dealings with North Korea. In April, South Korea announced it was giving up its effort to exchange special envoys with the North. In early May, Kim Young Sam warned North Korea that it would suffer self-destruction if it continued to develop nuclear weapons. And in late May, South Korean leaders threatened to reconsider the 1992 North-South denuclearization agreement, while calling for thorough preparedness against North Korea. Following a breakdown in negotiations between Pyongyang and the IAEA and a North Korean decision to remove the fuel rods at its major nuclear reactor, Kim Young Sam and Clinton agreed in June to seek sanctions against North Korea in the United Nations.

For its part, the U.S. suspended efforts to resume negotiations with North Korea in light of the intensely negative reaction in South Korea to the "sea of fire" statement. Although President Clinton emphasized that the U.S. did not want to

---

[26] Sigal (1998), p. 105.

escalate tensions with North Korea, he subsequently sent Kim Young Sam a personal message reaffirming the U.S. security commitment, which the Pentagon backed up by deploying 192 Patriot missiles to South Korea. As the North Koreans moved to reprocess the spent fuel from its Yongbyon reactor in the late spring, the U.S. turned actively to consider military options for dealing with the North Korean nuclear challenge.[27]

Jimmy Carter's visit to Pyongyang in mid-June put a plug in this downward spiral insofar as the U.S. was concerned. By securing Kim Il Sung's agreement to freeze all North Korean activities at its nuclear facilities, Carter cut off the U.S. moves toward both economic sanctions and military steps that risked a major conflict. And by acquiring Kim Il Sung's imprimatur on the negotiation of a broader agreement that would end the nuclear dimension of North Korea's military threat, he helped initiate a process that led four months later to the U.S.-DPRK Agreed Framework. As noted above, the Agreed Framework formalized the indefinite freeze on North Korea's overt nuclear program and allowed international inspections of its existing nuclear plants in exchange for two light water reactors, 500,000 tons of heavy fuel oil annually, and other political and economic commitments. This largely ended the crisis in U.S.-North Korean relations.

It did not, however, end the tensions in U.S.-South Korean relations. Part of the reason related to the nature of interactions between the two Koreas themselves. In a further effort to get South Korea into the game, on June 18 Kim Young Sam once again proposed a North-South summit meeting. One day after final agreement had been reached on procedural issues related to the summit, however, Kim Il Sung suddenly passed away. Two days later North Korea formally postponed the summit. When Kim Young Sam not only refused to offer condolences to North Koreans on the death of their leader but also prohibited other South Koreans from making their own statements of regret, North Korea cut off all substantive interactions with the ROK government. It then refused to deal with the Kim Young Sam administration for the remainder of its term (except on issues related to food assistance). With U.S.-DPRK negotiations moving actively ahead over the summer and fall, South Korean annoyance mounted steadily.

Another part of the reason for the growing tensions in U.S.-ROK relations though had to do with the Agreed Framework itself. To be sure, most South Koreans welcomed the freeze on North Korea's nuclear program, and they were pleased

---

[27] For an insider's account, see former Secretary of Defense Perry's description of this process in Carter and Perry (1999), pp. 124–133.

with the Framework's requirement that North Korea take steps to implement the North-South Joint Denuclearization Declaration and engage in North-South dialogue. But they had two major concerns with the substance of the agreement itself.

One, shared by many in the U.S. as well, had to do with the lack of any requirement for full North Korean compliance with IAEA requirements. The Agreed Framework only contained a vague North Korean pledge to "eventually dismantle" its nuclear reactors and to come into full compliance with its safeguards agreement "when a significant portion of the LWR project is completed, but before delivery of key components." This postponed special inspections of North Korean nuclear facilities for at least five years. Many South Koreans were aghast and felt that the U.S. was being duped by North Korea. Kim Young Sam himself was derisive, publicly criticizing the U.S. for its "lack of knowledge" and "over-eagerness to compromise."[28]

The other concern was even bigger. Although U.S. officials have often stressed that the only American commitments were to organize an international consortium to build the light water reactors and to provide North Korea supplies of heavy fuel oil, in fact the wording of the Agreed Framework conveyed a far more central role. The text of the Framework says, for example, *the U.S. will undertake to make arrangements*" for the light water reactor project and "will organize *under its leadership* an international consortium" to finance and supply these reactors [emphases added]. It also says "the U.S., *representing the international consortium, will serve as the principal point of contact with the DPRK for the LWR project*" [emphasis added]. Never once does the text mention South Korea or identify any South Korean role in the entire project. Even worse, from a South Korean perspective, the Agreed Framework commits the U.S. to "move toward full normalization of political and economic relations" with North Korea (Section II) without any *preconditions* of a comparable normalization in inter-Korean relations (Section III simply commits the North to "engage in North-South dialogue"). Indeed, the Agreed Framework lacks a target date—or even general timeframe—for improved North-South relations.[29]

---

[28] "We have spoken with North Korea more than 400 times," Kim said. "It didn't get us anywhere. They are not sincere. The important thing is that the United States should not be led on by the manipulations of North Korea." Sterngold (1994). This citation and broader account is drawn from Snyder (1999), pp. 112–113.

[29] Oberdorfer (2001), pp. 355-356. U.S. insistence on inclusion of a clause committing North Korea to resume North-South dialogue, preferably with at least some kind of general timetable phrase (e.g., "by such and such date" or "at the earliest time"), was linked to Kim Young Sam's vehement opposition to the draft accord. According to Oberdorfer, North Korea strongly resisted any such inclusion, however, and ultimately agreed only to the vague formulation ("will engage in North-South dialogue, as this Agreed Framework will help create an atmosphere that promotes such

The reaction of most elite groups and public opinion in general to the Agreed Framework was strongly negative. Not only was the U.S. dealing with South Korea's "evil twin," as one observer put it, but it was doing so "behind South Korea's back."[30] This negative reaction should not have been surprising. South Koreans' frustration at being cut out of the process and relegated to a clearly subordinate position had been mounting for some time, as had their unease with the U.S.-DPRK negotiating process. This was reflected in South Korea's decision to send a high-ranking ambassador to the Geneva negotiations to monitor the U.S.-North Korean negotiations that produced the October 1994 Agreed Framework.[31] It also was reflected in South Korea's adamant position that the ROK must have a central role in any project to build new nuclear reactors in North Korea. For example:

- On August 28 the South Korean government stated categorically that it would not take part in the LWR project unless a South Korean model was adopted for construction.

- On September 22 Kim sent another personal message to Clinton saying that, if North Korea's nuclear transparency was ensured, South Korea wanted to play a central role in the LWR project.

- When North Korea said it would not accept a South Korean model for its light water reactors two days later, Kim Young Sam became so agitated that he publicly criticized the U.S. for negotiating an agreement which, among other things, included an explicit requirement for North-South dialogue.[32]

In the wake of the U.S.-DPRK accord, South Korea shifted its policy in November 1994 to one that did not link South Korean assistance and other cooperation to the North Korean nuclear problem. It retained, however, its emphasis on a central role for the ROK in the LWR project. Addressing this strong South Korean desire became a focus of attention for the rest of 1994 and first half of 1995, as the U.S. and North Korea held a series of negotiations on protocols to implement the Agreed Framework. It also became an additional source of tension between South Korea and the U.S. By May 1995 the two were holding bilateral security meetings in Seoul every other week, in addition to nearly monthly consultations at the foreign minister and deputy foreign minister level and regular trilateral talks between the U.S., South Korea, and Japan. Virtually

---

dialogue") contained in the final text. The North subsequently used this formulation as an excuse not to fulfill its commitment.

[30] Ibid., p. 358.

[31] Snyder (1999), p. 109.

[32] "If the United States wants to settle with a half-baked compromise," he added, "...they can. But I think it would bring more danger and peril." Ibid., pp. 112–113.

all of these meetings included some discussion and/or reaffirmation of South Korea's role in the LWR project and importance of resuming inter-Korean dialogue—none of which did much to assuage South Korean annoyance over its exclusion from the negotiating process.

North Korea, naturally, was not helpful, refusing throughout this period to allow any formal South Korean role in the LWR project. On September 24, 1994 for example, the DPRK stated categorically that it would not accept South Korean models for its light water reactors. On January 16, 1995 it announced that the Agreed Framework would be endangered if it were supplied with South Korean reactors. An on March 11 the North threatened not to recognize the Korean Peninsula Energy Development Organization (KEDO), the international consortium established by the U.S. as part of its obligations under the Agreed Framework, if the U.S. kept insisting on a South Korean model for the light water reactors.

Instead, North Korea focused on trying to inflame political tensions inside South Korea, proposing among other things a meeting of political parties from both sides to discuss joint "National Liberation Day" activities and the formation of a South-North government. The regime also refused to resume inter-Korean dialogue, although it did agree to meet with South Korean representatives in mid-June 1995 to discuss a ROK offer of free rice. Even then Pyongyang made trouble. When the first South Korean vessel bearing the rice aid arrived in North Korea later that month, North Korean officials required the vessel to raise the North Korean flag, setting off a huge political firestorm in South Korea and temporary suspension of South Korean rice shipments.

On June 12, 1995 U.S. and North Korean negotiators reached agreement in Kuala Lumpur on provisions for implementing the Agreed Framework.[33] These provisions reiterated that KEDO would operate "under U.S. leadership" and that, "as specified in the Agreed Framework, the U.S. will serve as the principal point of contact with the DPRK for the LWR project." Spelling this out further, the provisions stipulated that "U.S. citizens will lead delegations and teams of KEDO as required to fulfill this role" and that "a U.S. firm will serve as program coordinator to assist KEDO in supervising overall implementation of the LWR project." The reaction of many South Koreans to these provisions was generally between irritation and anger. This time period, as we will see in Chapter 3, marked a low point in Korean attitudes toward the U.S.

---

[33] The text of the agreement, titled "Joint U.S.-DPRK Press Statement, Kuala Lumpur, June 13, 1995," is available online at http://www.kedo.org.

The agreement did succeed, however, in getting South Korea into the game. Using artful wording, the agreement stipulated that the reactor model to be used in the LWR project "will be the advanced version of U.S.-origin design and technology currently under production." It also granted to KEDO the authority to select both this model and the prime contractor to carry out the project. The following day (June 13) President Clinton sent President Kim Young Sam another personal letter reconfirming previous U.S. assurances that the reactor model KEDO would select would be a South Korean model (which is in fact an "advanced version of U.S.-origin design and technology currently under production"). The letter also reassured Kim that South Korea would play a key role in the LWR project. "Key role" was widely understood to mean that South Korea would serve as lead contractor in the project, a decision formally ratified in March 1996 when KEDO designated a South Korean power company (KEPCO) as lead contractor.

If the Agreed Framework effectively ended debate over how to respond to North Korea's nuclearization—the first major issue raised by North Korea's threat to withdraw from the NPT in March 1993—the Kuala Lumpur talks on provisions for implementing the Agreed Framework resolved the second issue: what South Korea's role would be in the LWR project. While many South Koreans were still upset about the ROK's decidedly second-class status and perceived subordination of South Korea's interests to the "global" interests of the United States, the government was relieved that South Korea would have a major role in the reactor construction process. This still left unresolved, however, the issue of South Korea's broader role in inter-Korean matters and, more specifically, the connection between U.S. dealings with North Korea and progress in North-South relations.

On this issue there remained considerable bad feeling in South Korea. South Koreans had taken seriously U.S. emphasis during the Reagan and Bush administrations on South Korea having the "lead" role on inter-Korean matters and many resented—especially in the context of the historic 1992 North-South agreements—what they considered to be U.S. trampling on their turf. They chafed in particular over perceived U.S. willingness to move forward in relations with North Korea despite Pyongyang's continuing refusal to deal directly and responsibly with the ROK.

This annoyance was evident during Kim Young Sam's next trip to Washington in July 1995, only one month after the Kuala Lumpur accord. In a speech to a joint session of Congress Kim suggested that "peace on the Korean Peninsula can only take root through dialogue and cooperation between the South and the North, the two parties directly concerned. Without dialogue, nothing can be accomplished."[34] Just in case the point might be missed, Kim underlined it by expressing his gratitude "that the President and Congress have stressed the central importance of South-North dialogue."

The basic issue was not resolved, however, until the April 1996 U.S.-ROK summit meeting in Cheju, Korea when President Clinton agreed to jointly propose a "Four Party Meeting" of the two Koreas, the U.S., and China as a means for encouraging greater North-South reconciliation. According to the text of the joint U.S.-ROK statement announcing this agreement:[35]

- The two presidents "confirmed the fundamental principle that establishment of a stable, permanent peace on the Korean Peninsula is the task of the Korean people."

- They agreed that "South and North Korea should take the lead in a renewed search for a permanent peace arrangement."

- And they stressed that "separate negotiations between the United States and North Korea on peace-related issues can not be considered."

With this joint statement, a basis was laid for alleviating the strains in U.S.-ROK relations. In certain respects, the two countries had come full circle. But it is hard to exaggerate the reverberations inside a newly democratizing South Korea of the process involved in getting there. The Kim Young Sam government bounced back and forth. With the twin objectives of ending the North Korean nuclear program and ensuring the ROK a central role in the process, it alternately tried to entice and ignore North Korea, to encourage and restrain the United States, and to both lead and follow South Korean public opinion. Domestic political considerations heavily influenced the government's actions as the mood of the South Korean public swung widely from event to event.

Accordingly, the character of leadership statements also fluctuated. From the latter part of 1992, and especially prior to the Agreed Framework, South Korean leaders repeatedly stressed the gravity of the North Korean nuclear threat and importance of North-South dialogue. They equally repeatedly sought, and emphasized, U.S. reassurances concerning its security commitment and military presence in Korea, as well as concerning the centrality of the South Korean role on inter-Korean matters. These emphases, together with repeated calls from President Kim on down for close policy coordination, communicated an

---

[34] "Address by President Kim Young-Sam of Korea at a Joint Session of the U.S. Congress," July 26, 1995. A text of the speech is in Yonhap News Agency, *Korea Annual 1996*, pp. 360–362.

[35] "Korea-U.S. Joint Announcement Between Presidents Kim Young-Sam and Bill Clinton," April 16, 1996. Ibid., p. 363.

awareness of the fundamental importance of the U.S.-ROK relationship. But they also communicated a sense of significant policy divergence between South Korea and the United States, as well as a palpable distrust of U.S. intentions. These latter communications tended to be particularly pronounced in periods associated with extensive U.S.-North Korean interactions, such as the periods around finalization of the Agreed Framework in October 1994 and its implementing provisions in June 1995.

For their part, the media were merciless in their criticism of the government. Much of this criticism was focused on the government's alleged incompetence and lack of diplomatic capability. Such criticism reached a peak when North Korea threatened to turn Seoul into a "sea of fire," with South Korean media accusing the government of sitting idly by during the greatest security threat since the Korean war.[36] Many mainstream media used the government's alleged failure to manage North Korea policy as a metaphor for larger failings in conducting national affairs. They castigated the Kim Young Sam administration in particular for having to rely excessively on U.S. diplomatic assistance. Along with their principal focus on the South Korean government, the media also mixed in frequent warnings for the U.S. not to be naïve about North Korea or overlook important South Korean interests in its dealings with Pyongyang.

The opposition parties generally echoed these themes. Although Kim Dae Jung's party strongly opposed any consideration of sanctions and insisted on a "peaceful" resolution of the nuclear issue, it joined with the other opposition parties in criticizing the government's inconsistency and berating its competence. A frequent theme was the alleged lack of an "independent" South Korean policy.

Not surprisingly, all this affected public opinion as well, with South Korean attitudes toward the U.S. deteriorating significantly. As indicated in Chapter 3 (see Figure 3.3), for example, those South Koreans expressing a favorable opinion of the U.S. plummeted from 67 percent at the height of the nuclear crisis in October 1993 to 43 percent in June 1995. Positive views of the U.S.-ROK relationship showed a similar decline in this period.

Although the nuclear crisis dominated events, it was not of course the only important development. Many other things were happening that influenced South Korean attitudes toward the U.S. Among these two stand out. One had to do with continuing North Korean military provocations. Some of these, such as North Korean efforts to undermine the truce arrangements in the spring of 1994, were mostly annoying. Others, such as the repeated incursions by hundreds of

---

[36]Kim (1999), p. 232.

heavily armed North Korean troops into the Joint Security Area of the DMZ in early April 1996, were more worrisome.

The most important provocation, however, had to do with the grounding of a North Korean submarine on South Korea's eastern coast in September 1996.[37] This incident, which precipitated a massive, two-week South Korean manhunt and the deaths of two dozen North Korean commandos (along with more than a dozen South Korean soldiers), set off a firestorm of criticism in South Korea. In response, the South Korean government cut off all dealings with the North, suspended its activities in KEDO, and threatened to withdraw both its "Four Party" talks proposal and participation in the LWR project. U.S. efforts to walk a line between showing solidarity with its South Korean ally and maintaining its nuclear agreement—and budding relationship—with the DPRK infuriated both South Korean leaders and public alike and intensified the negative reaction in South Korea. South Koreans were particularly irate over a comment by U.S. Secretary of State Warren Christopher that urged "all parties" to avoid further provocations. By implying not only equivalence between South Korea and the North but also U.S. equidistance between the two Koreas, the comment raised questions in South Korea about the reliability of the United States and broader value of the U.S.-ROK alliance. While a package accord negotiated at the Kim-Clinton summit meeting in November kept both U.S.-ROK and U.S.-DPRK relations from unraveling, hard feelings toward the U.S. in South Korea lingered.

The other major development during this period had to do with U.S. economic policy—specifically, the strong U.S. pressure on South Korea to further open its markets. To be sure, this was not new. The U.S. had begun to increase market-opening pressure back in the second half of the 1980s, based on the belief that the chronic U.S. trade deficit was largely a result of trade barriers on the part of Asian countries. Nor was the development unique to South Korea. Japan and other Asian trading partners had, along with the European Union, long been targets of "voluntary export restraints," "Super 301" legislation, and other neo-protectionist provisions of U.S. trade law. But under President Clinton, the U.S. took a more assertive, even confrontational, approach to international economic negotiations and explicitly sought to recast the entire intellectual basis of U.S. trade policy to locate trade more at the center of U.S. foreign policy.[38]

In the case of South Korea, this policy manifested itself in strong market-opening pressure, particularly in the agricultural and automotive sectors. Many South

---

[37]For a good account, see Oberdorfer (2001), pp. 387–393.

[38]Garten (1993), available online at http://www.foreignaffairs.org.

Korean leaders understood that it was in Korea's own interest to liberalize its markets. Many other South Koreans, however, insisted that the ROK could never compete with the United States and harshly criticized the U.S. for its alleged "bullying" approach. Kim Young Sam's public apology to the nation on December 9, 1993 for failing to thwart the opening of South Korea's rice market, after President Clinton rejected his personal appeal to two days earlier, captures an important aspect of the domestic political mood at the time. The ROK's limited ability to resist U.S. trade pressures given the large disparity in the two countries' economies and importance of the U.S. market to South Korea reinforced growing resentment over South Korea's dependence on the United States.

The Inter-Korean Summit (2000–2002)

The atmosphere in U.S.-ROK relations at the end of the 1990s could hardly have been more different from that of the earlier part of the decade. Kim Dae Jung's inauguration in February 1998—the first time a leader of the political opposition had ever become president in South Korea—brought with it a new South Korean leadership with significantly different policy orientations. Among other important differences with his predecessor, Kim's active encouragement of U.S. dealings with North Korea as part of his Sunshine Policy of engagement contributed to a marked lessening in U.S.-ROK tensions.

President Clinton's appointment of former Secretary of Defense William Perry to be special advisor and policy coordinator for North Korea in November 1998 reinforced this trend. Perry's full-scale review of U.S. policy toward North Korea and active efforts to synchronize U.S. policy with that of South Korea (the so-called "Perry process") restored a sense of coherence to U.S. policy and commonality to U.S. and South Korean approaches.[39] Strong U.S. support for South Korea's own engagement with North Korea created a sense of compatibility in U.S. and ROK policies that hadn't existed since the early 1990s.

South Korea's experience with the financial crisis of 1997–1998 played a critical role as well. Not only did the crisis put North Korea on the back burner, as most South Koreans turned inward to focus on their immediate economic situations, it also had a healing effect on U.S.-ROK relations by identifying the U.S. as part of

---

[39] The appointment of Perry came after opposition to the administration's North Korea policy swelled in Congress in the wake of North Korea's long-range missile test and construction of an underground facility suspected of being designed for nuclear weapons production in August 1998. The prospect of North Korean nuclear weapons despite the Agreed Framework and the long-range missiles to deliver them challenged both the assumptions underlying U.S. policy and the political support necessary to sustain it.

the solution to this paramount South Korean problem. This identification strengthened as the South Korean economy demonstrated strong growth—and a remarkably rapid recovery—in 1999 and 2000. Notwithstanding early laments by some South Koreans about the allegedly U.S.-led "IMF crisis," the U.S. role during the financial crisis actually had a salutary effect on both South Korean attitudes toward the U.S. and U.S.-South Korean relations. This is reflected in polls showing the percentage of South Koreans expressing a favorable opinion of the U.S. rising from 61 percent in April 1998 to 71 percent in May 2000, with those expressing an unfavorable opinion declining from 36 percent to 27 percent in the same period. Indeed, by the beginning of 2000 many observers considered the U.S.-ROK relationship to have never been better.[40]

The historic summit meeting between South Korean President Kim Dae Jung and North Korean leader Kim Jong Il in June 2000 appeared to strengthen the relationship further. The warmth of the welcome South Korean delegates received in Pyongyang and range of areas agreed upon for cooperative efforts created the impression of a truly momentous breakthrough in inter-Korean reconciliation. The equally historic initiation of North-South family reunions—which began in August for the first time since the Korean War—and opening ceremonies of the 2000 Olympics in September—during which athletes from both Koreas marched under a single flag—reinforced this impression. Among other significant effects discussed below, these developments helped restore a sense that South Koreans were actively involved in determining their own future and reduced both animosities toward the U.S. and anxieties about continuing U.S.-North Korean interactions.

For its part, the U.S. expressed its unqualified support for the summit meeting from the time of its announcement and repeated this support frequently. It also praised Kim Dae Jung personally for his wisdom and long-term vision and strongly endorsed his government's engagement policy.[41] The U.S. reinforced this verbal support by stepping up its own dealings with North Korea. The Clinton administration moved to ease sanctions against North Korea in mid-June, for example, and restarted missile talks with North Korean negotiators in early July. In October North Korean General Jo Myong-rok and U.S. Secretary of State Madeline Albright exchanged visits, which produced among other things a joint commitment to end hostility between the two countries. Although agreement on a missile deal that would enable President Clinton to visit North

---

[40] See, for example, Brown (1999), available online at http://www.csis.org/pacfor.

[41] President Clinton went on to laud the summit as testimony to U.S. success at continually insisting upon inter-Korean dialogue. Noerper (2000), available at http://www.csis.org/pacfor.

Korea before his term expired was not achieved, the high-level visits and parallel working-level talks in Kuala Lumpur marked the first substantive progress in six years of U.S.-DPRK negotiations over the North's missile program. They also suggested the possibility of a different kind of U.S. relationship with North Korea.

The South Korean government strongly encouraged these efforts. Seeing improved U.S.-DPRK relations as essential to furthering inter-Korean reconciliation, President Kim personally urged President Clinton to visit North Korea when the two met at the APEC meeting in mid-November. South Korea also moved aggressively to implement its commitments under the summit agreements by hosting a North-South Defense Ministerial Meeting in September and beginning construction of its side of the agreed-upon North-South railroad. Separately, President Kim reaffirmed the importance of the U.S.-ROK alliance and vital role played by U.S. military forces on the Korean Peninsula.

On the bilateral front, the U.S. and South Korea cooperated actively to resolve long-standing irritants in the security relationship. The agreements on extending the range and payload of South Korean missiles in October and on revising the Status of Forces Agreement (SOFA) in December were particularly important in this regard. These agreements not only defused two politically explosive issues. They also helped nurture a greater public sense of U.S. "respect" for South Korean interests.

The North-South summit thus had beneficial effects overall on U.S.-ROK relations. It also planted two seeds, however, of future tensions. One had to do with the issue of what priority to place on economic cooperation and humanitarian exchanges versus on steps to reduce the nuclear and other threats from North Korea. Even before the summit there was some divergence between Washington and Seoul on this issue, with the U.S. urging South Korea to place threat reduction measures higher on its inter-Korean agenda. The outcome of the summit reinforced this divergence. Not only did the Joint Declaration fail to address any of the pressing military issues it didn't even mention the words "peace" and "security" at all.[42]

The second seed planted during the summit had to do with the best approach for effectuating change in North Korea. Shortly before the summit the South Korean government formally jettisoned any strict conditionality or requirement for reciprocity in its dealings with the North, arguing that South Korea—as the

---

[42] The text of the Joint Declaration is available online at the ROK Ministry of Unification's web site, http://www.unikorea.go.kr/.

stronger "elder brother"—should be patient and allow North Korea to reciprocate South Korean measures in its own time.[43] The summit's success reinforced the government's view that this is the best approach to take with a state as prickly and insecure as North Korea. Such was not generally the case with many Americans, who are more legalistic by nature and more distrustful of North Korean intentions by experience. Both in the missile talks in the second half of 2000 and in broader U.S.-DPRK interactions, the U.S. maintained clear linkages between concessions on its part and concrete changes in North Korean policy.

One more immediate effect of the summit was to further reduce the already declining sense of external threat inside South Korea. This was to some extent inevitable, given the dramatic images displayed on South Korean television screens of North Korea's respectful reception of the South Korean delegation and seemingly reasonable demeanor. But President Kim also helped foster this effect in his effort to achieve inter-Korean reconciliation, which he believed would not be possible without changing the view that South Koreans have always had North Korea. Accordingly, he actively urged South Koreans to think of North Korea and its people not as "enemies" seeking to conquer South Korea but as "brothers and sisters" needing South Korean help. As he put it on his return to Seoul following the historic summit:

> The Pyongyang people are the same as us, the same nation sharing the same blood. Regardless of what they have been saying and [how they have been] acting outwardly, they have deep love and a longing for their compatriots in the South. If you talk with them, you notice that right away…. We must consider North Koreans as our brothers and sisters. We must believe that they have the same thought…. Most importantly there is no longer going to be any war. The North will no longer attempt unification by force and at the same time we will not do any harm to the North….[44]

Aware of the potentially adverse impact of declining threat perceptions on South Korea's broader security interests Kim strongly and repeatedly emphasized the importance of the U.S.-ROK alliance. He also stressed the need for close U.S.-ROK security cooperation. Warning of the power vacuum that would be created were the U.S. to withdraw its forces, Kim called for a continued U.S. military presence in Korea even after unification. The South Korean government actively spread the word that Kim made this latter point to Kim Jong Il as well during their summit talks, adding that the North Korean leader responded by

---

[43]Young-shik (1998), pp. 54–55.

[44] For the full text of his remarks, see "President Kim Dae Jung's Remarks on Returning to Seoul from the Inter-Korean Summit in Pyongyang," *The Korea Herald*, June 16, 2000.

acknowledging the point and indicating he accepts a continued U.S. military presence in Korea.

Notwithstanding these public and private emphases, general South Korean threat perceptions predictably declined further after the summit. This decline helped erode the rationale on which the U.S.-ROK alliance has always rested—the need to deter and/or defeat aggression from a strong and threatening North Korea—and to some extent the perceived importance of the U.S. security presence. Together with Kim's broader approach to engagement, it also contributed over time to a domestic political climate increasingly intolerant of anti-North Korean actions—or even of public criticism of Kim Jong Il.[45]

The first summit meeting between President George W. Bush and President Kim in March 2001 came in this context and changed the tenor of U.S.-ROK relations almost overnight. Although President Kim appeared to achieve most of his main policy objectives, and gained the additional distinction of being the first leader from Asia invited to the White House, the summit meeting was almost universally portrayed as a diplomatic disaster.[46] This was largely because of a couple of off-hand comments President Bush made to the press. In these comments, Bush expressed his deep distrust of Kim Jong Il and belief in the need for reciprocity and adequate verification of any missile agreement with North Korea. Sharing his personal doubts that this would be possible given the nature of the North Korean system, moreover, he indicated that his administration would not resume missile talks with North Korea until it had completed its review of U.S. policy.

These comments, aided by sensationalist media treatment on the South Korean side, actively fostered the impression in South Korea that the stalemate then existing in North-South relations (North Korea had put substantive progress on hold prior to the summit) was due to the policies of the new U.S. administration. North Korea just as actively reinforced this impression, denouncing the U.S. for trying to prevent inter-Korean reconciliation. The long delay in completing the U.S. policy review (over five months) contributed by conveying a sense that the U.S. was, at a minimum, not overly concerned about the lack of progress in North-South relations.

The outcome of the policy review in June 2001 was generally a reiteration of the main message emerging from the March summit. Put simply: The U.S. would continue to support South Korea's engagement policy and seek its own serious

---

[45]Kim (2002).

[46] For details, see Levin and Han (2002), pp. 107–112.

dialogue with North Korea, but its approach would be more cautious than that of South Korea and more focused on critical security issues. Specifically, the U.S. announced it would pursue an open, unconditional, and enhanced dialogue with North Korea while maintaining the Agreed Framework. But in pursuing such a dialogue the U.S. would adopt a "comprehensive approach" designed to address a "broad agenda" of issues, including "improved implementation of the Agreed Framework," "verifiable constraints" on North Korea's missile programs and ban on its missile exports, and a "less threatening conventional military posture."[47]

Supporters of the Sunshine Policy in Seoul had a generally mixed reaction to this U.S. message. While they were relieved that the Bush Administration had decided to continue pursuing dialogue with North Korea, they were concerned that its insistence on expanding the agenda—especially to conventional issues—would alienate Pyongyang and cause it to step back from expanded interactions. Many saw the emphases on verifiability of new agreements and improved implementation of existing ones as implicit criticisms of South Korea's own approach and suspected that slowing down North-South progress was the real U.S. intention. The U.S. message received an even worse hearing in Pyongyang. Ignoring the repeated U.S. emphasis on open, "unconditional" talks, North Korea accused the U.S. of trying to put "conditions" on the resumption of negotiations and rebuffed the offer. It also refused for several more months to resume North-South dialogue.[48]

A series of statements and actions by the Bush Administration in the months after the terrorist attacks of September 11, 2001 strengthened the sense among South Korean critics of U.S. policy that the Bush Administration was out to "get" rather than "deal with" North Korea. For example:

- As the global war on terrorism got under way in mid-October President Bush publicly warned North Korea not to doubt the U.S. resolve to defend South Korea or try to take advantage of U.S. involvement in Afghanistan. To back up the warning, the U.S. deployed additional fighter aircraft to South Korea to compensate for the deployment of a U.S. aircraft carrier away from the North Pacific to South Asia.

---

[47] The text of the official statement by President Bush is available online at http://www.whitehouse.gov.

[48] In the midst of a no-confidence vote in the ROK National Assembly against the architect of the sunshine policy, Lim Dong-Won, in September 2001, North Korea broke its six-month long refusal to deal with or even respond to South Korea by suddenly proposing new inter-Korean ministerial talks. This proposal, widely seen in South Korea as a transparent North Korean attempt to influence the outcome of the National Assembly vote, backfired. President Kim's coalition government split and the vote passed, bringing down the South Korean government.

- A couple days later President Bush publicly criticized Kim Jong Il—which some South Koreans saw as coming close to taunting—for his "timidity" in not taking up the U.S. offer of a serious dialogue.

- In late November President Bush demanded that North Korea accept international inspections of its suspected weapons of mass destruction activities and end its destabilizing sale of missiles and missile technology.

- In mid-December the U.S. formally withdrew from the Anti-Ballistic Missile treaty, warning of the danger from "rogue" states—a term used widely for years to describe countries like North Korea but formally dropped by former Secretary of State Albright in June 2000—seeking weapons of mass destruction.

- In early January 2002 the Pentagon completed its Nuclear Posture Review which called for the development of new nuclear and other earth-penetrating weapons better suited to hit underground targets and identified a range of contingencies for which such weapons might be used, all of which applied explicitly to North Korea.[49]

- In late January President Bush formally elevated North Korea to the pantheon of regimes—the so-called "axis of evil"—deemed to pose a "grave and growing danger" to the United States.[50]

- And in March President Bush refused to certify North Korean adherence to the Agreed Framework for the first time since its signing, signaling growing U.S. concern about Pyongyang's nuclear activities and intention to do something about them.

For its part, North Korea responded to U.S. rhetoric by ratcheting up its own rhetoric. Portraying the U.S. as preparing to launch an attack on North Korea and having moved the situation on the Korean peninsula to the brink of war, it denounced the U.S. proposal for dialogue as a sham and called for a military buildup to meet the U.S. threat. Matching actions to words, it once again broke off North-South talks in November—which had only resumed in mid September—with no agreement or date for meeting again. By March 2002 North Korea was calling U.S. leaders "nuclear lunatics" and threatening to reexamine all previous agreements with the U.S., including the Agreed Framework.

All this generated new fears of war inside South Korea and growing dismay within the government over the reluctance of the U.S. to find a way to save

---

[49] U.S. Department of Defense, *Nuclear Posture Review*, January 8, 2002, p. 16.

[50] "The President's State of the Union Address," January 29, 2002. A copy is available at http://www.whitehouse.gov.

North Korea's "face" and resume U.S.-DPRK dialogue. More subtly, it stimulated latent South Korean sensitivities about their fate being determined by outside powers. Many South Koreans understood U.S. rhetoric as suggesting, as one foreign observer living in Seoul put it at the time, that "the U.S. was ready to attack North Korea at the cost of thwarting Korea's long-term process of reunification."[51] A good number of these same South Koreans, moreover, heard statements like "The United States of America will not permit the world's most dangerous regimes to threaten us with the world's most dangerous weapons" as implying that the U.S. was prepared to move unilaterally whatever South Korea's interests.

To be sure, this period in U.S.-ROK relations was not all negative. President Kim expressed South Korea's full support for the U.S. war on terrorism after 9/11 and contributed a small but symbolically important military support package to assist U.S. activities in Afghanistan. For his part, President Bush repeated his strong support for President Kim's Sunshine Policy during his trip to Seoul in February 2002. In a further effort to calm anxieties in Seoul caused by his "axis of evil" comment, he also publicly ruled out any U.S. military invasion of North Korea. Reiterating the U.S. proposal for unconditional talks with Pyongyang, Bush separately urged South Korea and China to impress on North Korean leaders the sincere U.S. desire for dialogue. These mutual efforts helped narrow the gap between U.S. and ROK approaches and lower the temperature somewhat in U.S.-ROK relations.

Still, it would be a mistake to downplay the impact in South Korea of the U.S. statements and other actions during this period. Supporters of the Sunshine Policy angrily accused the U.S. of provoking war and warned the U.S. not to undermine South Korean foreign policy. Some ruling party politicians and parts of the South Korean press suggested that the U.S. was sabotaging North-South interactions.[52] One representative of Kim Dae Jung's ruling party temporarily paralyzed National Assembly proceedings by calling Bush himself "evil incarnate."[53] Opponents of government policy, on the other hand, charged that the Kim Dae Jung administration was endangering both U.S.-ROK relations and South Korean security.

One clear effect of all this was to strengthen the sharp ideological cleavage in South Korean politics and exacerbate the task of reaching consensus on policy

---

[51]Gross (2002), available at http://www.csis.org/pacfor.

[52] For a more extended account of South Korean intimations that the U.S. was trying to undermine ROK-DPRK relations, see Eberstadt (2002), especially pp. 155–157.

[53]Hyung Jin (2002).

toward North Korea. Another less obvious effect was to stimulate an incipient shift in the popular image of the U.S. from a protector of South Korea's security to a potential impediment to inter-Korean reconciliation. Some South Koreans, especially among the younger generations, began to blame the U.S. more than North Korea for the growing tensions on the Korean peninsula.

Meanwhile, U.S.-ROK relations were beset by other difficulties throughout this period. On the economic side, a December 2001 decision by the U.S. International Trade Commission (ITC) to recommend tariffs on South Korean steel exports, adopted by President Bush in March 2002, irritated both government and public alike and induced South Korea to join with the European Union to develop countermeasures. U.S. dismissal of South Korean interest in a bilateral Free Trade Agreement on the grounds that South Korea had a long way to go first in opening its markets, while understandable on its merits, similarly stung South Korean opinion. A sharp slowdown in the South Korean economy in 2001 after rapid and sustained growth in 1999 and 2000 magnified the impact by fueling public anxieties about future economic prospects.

On the security side, a reported plan by U.S. Forces Korea (USFK) to build new housing on the Yongsan military base in the center of Seoul set off a sharp public reaction, particularly by parts of South Korea's newly emergent civic and non-governmental organizations (NGOs). So too did perceived U.S. pressure on South Korea to choose a U.S. aircraft for its next-term (FSX) fighter, which the government finally did in May 2002. But the big bombshell came in June when a U.S. military vehicle on a training exercise crushed two South Korean schoolgirls to death. This tragic incident stirred up enormous public antipathy toward the United States—particularly over the way the incident was handled—while re-opening broader societal fissures over the U.S. military role in Korea.

Such feelings were further stoked by a series of random events. The so-called "Ohno incident," in which a South Korean speed skater lost the gold medal to an American in the 2002 winter Olympics, was particularly important in this respect. Together with incessant media reporting of an off-color joke by comedian Jay Leno, which reinforced a widespread feeling that the U.S. "looks down on" South Koreans, the incident generated a strong outburst of nationalist sentiment. Soaring national pride in the wake of South Korea's remarkable performance in the World Cup games intensified the public reaction to these events. The perceived indifference of South Korean leaders to this upsurge in anti-American sentiment and early disinclination to defend the alliance in the face of massive public demonstrations further roiled both South Korean politics and the atmosphere in U.S.-ROK relations.

North Korea's unprovoked sinking of a South Korean naval vessel on June 29, 2002, which killed five sailors and injured many others, also sank what U.S. leaders subsequently described as a "bold approach" they had prepared to try and improve U.S.-North Korean relations. North Korea's statement of "regret" one month later set off a flurry of activity in North-South relations unparalleled since the months immediately following the June 2000 summit. Inter-ministerial talks were held, new family reunions were planned, and agreements were reached on a broad range of additional cooperative activities.

The suddenness of this activity, coming as it did with the clock running out on the Kim Dae Jung administration and amidst signs of potentially significant internal North Korean reforms, stimulated considerable discussion in South Korea about whether this time the North Korean regime might genuinely be ready to change. Japanese Prime Minister Koizumi's visit to Pyongyang at the height of all this activity in mid-September, which resulted in several dramatic North Korean gestures and progress on long-standing bilateral issues, reinforced this sense of incipient change. It also raised hopes among ROK government supporters for major progress in North-South relations.

A couple weeks later U.S. Assistant Secretary of State Kelly finally undertook his long delayed visit to Pyongyang. The original purpose of the visit was to explain to North Korean leaders the "bold approach" the U.S. had been planning. This approach would involve "significant economic and diplomatic steps to improve the lives of the North Korean people" if North Korea "dramatically altered its behavior" on issues of importance to the United States.[54] Kelly also informed the North Koreans, however, that the U.S. had irrefutable evidence that North Korea was conducting a program to enrich uranium for nuclear weapons in violation of multiple international commitments. When he explained that this kind of activity made such a "bold approach" impossible, the North Koreans first tried to gloss over the issue and then became defiant. Not only did they have such a program, they acknowledged, but they also considered the Agreed Framework nullified. Moreover, they insisted, they were entitled to possess not only nuclear weapons but even more powerful weapons.[55]

This marked the start of a further decline in U.S.-DPRK relations. In late October North Korea rejected international demands that it end its nuclear weapons program. In mid-November KEDO suspended shipments of heavy fuel oil to North Korea pending credible actions to dismantle its uranium enrichment

---

[54] "Statement by Assistant of Secretary of State for East Asian and Pacific Affairs James A. Kelly," October 19, 2002, available at http://usembassy.state.gov/seoul.

[55] "North Korea's Response," *The New York Times*, October 26, 2002.

program. In early December North Korea announced plans to reactivate its nuclear reactor frozen under the Agreed Framework. And at the end of December North Korea ordered IAEA inspectors to leave the country and physically dismantled their monitoring devices. In between the U.S., with the assistance of the Spanish navy, seized and inspected a North Korean naval vessel suspected of carrying illegal arms shipment before allowing it to resume its voyage. North Korea further escalated its rhetoric in response, calling among other things for South Koreans to join a sacred war against the United States and demanding compensation for U.S. "piracy."

All this fed a growing view in South Korea that the U.S. was trying to intimidate and isolate North Korea as a means to prevent inter-Korean reconciliation and eventually unification. It also led to increased efforts by South Korean activists to mobilize opinion against the United States. The continued U.S. insistence that it would not negotiate with Pyongyang until it honored its prior agreements was beginning to wear thin in this context. President Kim and other South Korean leaders, while echoing Washington's emphasis on full North Korean compliance with its nuclear commitments, became increasingly critical of the U.S. for refusing to begin negotiations and began to publicly call for changes in U.S.-South Korean relations. Roh Moo-Hyun's ability to capitalize on such sentiment was a significant factor in his election victory.

Although Roh indicated during the campaign (and reiterated more strongly after the election) that he supported the U.S.-ROK alliance and continued stationing of U.S. troops in South Korea, he made a number of other comments during the election campaign that undoubtedly helped roil public opinion. These include statements that he would not "kow-tow" to Washington and would insist upon a more "equal" U.S.-ROK relationship. Particularly problematic were comments implying that the U.S. was somehow unconcerned with South Korea's welfare and that the ROK might remain neutral in any U.S. conflict with North Korea.[56]

Although such comments were certainly idiosyncratic, they reflected a deeper difficulty South Korea had throughout this period in maintaining a balance between its security and unification objectives. They also reflected a growing gap between the U.S. and South Korea in their perceptions of the nature of North Korea and their assessments of the threat the regime poses. Whether priority should be placed on threat reduction measures or on economic and humanitarian cooperation and what the most effective approach is for effectuating change in North Korea were particularly contentious issues. By calling South Korea's

---

[56]Cossa (2002), available at http://www.csis.org/pacfor.

approach into question, these issues were perceived by many South Koreans as undercutting the government's policy and stimulated sensitivities about South Korea's fate once again being determined by outside powers. In this context, the year probably ended fittingly with President-elect Roh emphasizing that any U.S. policy decisions should fully consider South Korea's opinion.

History, the 1990s, and Factors Driving Korean Attitudes Toward the U.S.

This overview suggests something of the complexity of South Korean feelings about the United States. Gratitude, fondness, and respect mix in not always stable quantities with feelings of resentment and distrust. Widespread appreciation of the benefits South Korea receives from the U.S.-ROK alliance coexists uneasily at times with the annoyance many Koreans feel at their continuing dependence on the United States. In their sheer complexity, there is nothing in South Korean attitudes toward the U.S. fully comparable to South Korean attitudes toward their Japanese neighbors. Still, lingering suspicions about U.S. intentions and strong sensitivity toward U.S. policies or actions perceived as affecting South Korea's ability to control its own destiny constitute important residue from its historical experience with the United States.

Not surprisingly given the complexity of South Korean feelings and the inherent complexity of the U.S.-ROK relationship itself, South Korean attitudes have no single wellspring. They derive from many sources. In addition to the historical legacy, perceived security and economic conditions heavily influence South Korean feelings about the United States. Specific actions taken, or not taken, by both South Korea and the U.S. have critical impact as well, as do those of North Korea. Since the advent of democratization, the role of the media has come to play an increasingly important role in shaping South Korean opinion, as has social and generational change in South Korea more broadly. All this is depicted notionally in Figure 2.1. The shifting geopolitical scene around the Korean peninsula—with China becoming South Korea's largest trading partner and playing a critical role in trying to bring North Korea to the negotiating table, Russia joining the Six Party Talks and actively supporting South Korea's engagement strategy, and Japan being viewed especially by younger South Koreans in a more relaxed manner—heightens the complexity of both the current situation and evolving attitudes toward the United States.

This mixture of sources was evident in both of the periods in the 1990s in which there was significant movement in South Korean attitudes—the nuclear crisis of 1992–1996 and the period following the Inter-Korean summit of June 2000. In the period of the nuclear crisis between 1992 and 1996, one key factor influencing South Korean attitudes toward the United States had to do with fluctuations in South Korean threat perceptions and related views about the importance of the U.S. security role in Korea. This point needs to be stated with some care: Public opinion polls have consistently shown strong support for both the U.S.-ROK alliance and a continued U.S. military presence. Over the last 15 years, for example, the percentage of South Koreans who believe the presence of U.S. forces is important for protecting Korea's security has ranged between nine-tenths and three-fourths. Still, the polls show significant fluctuation in both directions, largely correlating with changes in the external threat environment.[57]

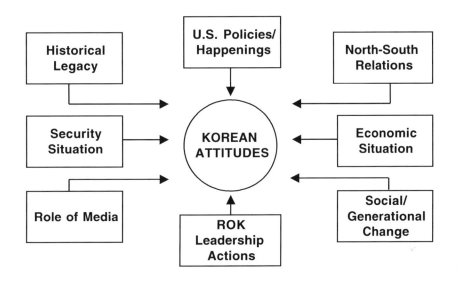

Figure 2.1—A Model of Influences on South Korean Attitudes Toward the U.S.

The second major factor driving South Korean attitudes in this period had to do with perceptions of the U.S. role on what was referred to above as "sovereignty-related issues." Nearly all South Koreans supported the goal of a non-nuclear North Korea and nearly as many welcomed the freeze on North Korean facilities worked out in U.S.-DPRK negotiations. But this freeze still left critical questions unresolved pertaining to South Korea's role in the LWR project and in inter-

[57] The 90 percent of South Koreans who believed the presence of U.S. forces was important for protecting Korea's security in July 1988, for example, fell to 78 percent in October 1991 as "Nordpolitik" advanced, the Soviet Union collapsed, and ROK "engagement" made strides with North Korea. This percentage went back up to 82-83 percent as the nuclear crisis unfolded in 1993 and then declined again to 72 percent in June 1995 after announcement of the Agreed Framework. The figure went back up again to 88 percent when North Korea ignored South Korea's Four Party Talks proposal and sent armed commandos into the South a year later and stayed in the upper half of the 80 percentile until after the historic June 2000 summit.

Korean matters more broadly. The resentment many South Koreans felt over what they perceived to be their second-class status—which the political leadership fanned rather than attempted to attenuate—and perceived subordination of South Korea's interests to the "global" interests of the United States helped drive their attitudes toward the U.S. during this period.

Undoubtedly there were many additional factors. North Korea, in its inimitable way, played a significant role by skillfully stoking a sense of South Korean subservience and impotence. The actions of the South Korean government in repeatedly staking out a hard line and then backing away when the U.S. took a softer or more conciliatory position probably also stimulated negative feelings. And the role of the media was clearly influential in fostering an impression of an overbearing, even disloyal U.S. and a ROK administration too feeble to stand up to the U.S. and protect South Korea's interests. U.S. economic pressures—particularly on politically sensitive issues like rice and autos—probably affected South Korean attitudes as well in this period.

The major factors driving South Korean attitudes toward the U.S. in the second period were rather similar. This is somewhat surprising: In certain respects the two periods were almost polar opposites. In the first period the U.S. was the central actor, with South Korea somewhere along the sidelines, whereas in the second period South Korea was the main protagonist and the U.S. played a supporting role (or did not). Similarly, whereas South Korea generally took the "hard line" toward North Korea in the first period and the U.S. adopted a softer, more accommodating position, the positions reversed in the second period. The kind of encouragement South Korea provided for U.S. interactions with the North in the second period had no analogue in the first. Still, the two major factors that appeared to drive South Korean attitudes in the initial period appear to have played a similar role in the latter period.

This seems clear in the case of the perceived importance of the U.S. security role. Even more so than the events of the Roh Tae-Woo period, the North-South summit significantly altered South Korean views of the North. As noted above, the Kim Dae Jung government actively facilitated this development by encouraging South Koreans to think of North Koreans not as enemies seeking to conquer South Korea but as "brothers and sisters" needing South Korean help. The summit also helped solidify a radical change in South Korean views of the desirable goal for South Korean policy: not precipitating its early demise but preventing its precipitate collapse. While concerns about the adverse impact such a collapse would have on the South Korean economy heavily influenced this change, a growing sense that North Korea no longer represented a significant threat also contributed. Both decreased the perceived need for a U.S. security guarantee and support for a large U.S. military presence.

The second major factor in the first period, South Korean perceptions of the U.S. role on sovereignty-related issues, also appears to have been a major factor driving South Korean attitudes toward the U.S. in the second period. The harsh language used by the Bush Administration to describe North Korea and its leader, coupled with what many South Koreans perceive as a reluctance to engage peacefully with North Korea, not only spawned new fears of war on the Korean peninsula but also fueled feelings that the U.S. does not take South Korean interests adequately into account when making its foreign policy decisions. These feelings were reinforced by clear differences over the appropriate priority for threat reduction measures as opposed to economic and humanitarian cooperation and over the most effective approach for effectuating change in North Korea. Even some South Koreans critics of the Sunshine Policy perceived U.S. positions on these issues as pulling the rug out from under the South Korean government. Such views reflected mounting South Korean frustration over the impasse in inter-Korean relations and stimulated long-standing sensitivities about South Korea's fate once again being determined by outside powers.

As in the first period, many other factors contributed to shaping South Korean attitudes. North Korea continued to play a role by holding progress in North-South relations hostage to U.S. concessions to Pyongyang, thereby strengthening a growing perception of the U.S. in certain South Korean circles as an impediment to inter-Korean reconciliation. The South Korean media also played a significant role, as did ruling party politicians and other supporters of the Sunshine Policy, by actively linking the stalemate in inter-Korean relations to U.S. policies toward North Korea. Participation by middle class citizens in massive demonstrations against the U.S. helped give "anti-American" sentiment a greater degree of legitimacy, which ROK government indifference facilitated.

In short, many factors helped drive South Korean attitudes toward the United States during the last decade. But the perceived importance of the U.S. security role and U.S. actions on ROK sovereignty-related issues appear to have been particularly influential.

In the next chapter, we turn from an historical approach to a quantitative one, and describe the key trends in South Korean attitudes toward the U.S. over the last decade.

3. Key Trends in South Korean Attitudes Toward the United States

The previous chapter identified a number of developments in the last decade that led to friction in the U.S.-South Korean bilateral relationship, and appear to have stimulated unfavorable attitudes toward the U.S. ranging from disappointment to mistrust, resentment, and even fear; the next chapter will examine the public opinion evidence for signs that the events and factors described in the last chapter had a discernible impact on South Koreans' attitudes.

The present chapter builds upon the last in a different way, by assessing whether the conventional wisdom is correct that there in fact has been a recent downturn in South Koreans' attitudes toward the U.S., as the historical record would suggest. To address this question we analyze the results from a wide variety of polling questions that have been asked about the U.S., the bilateral relationship, Americans, and other relevant topics. As will be shown, there is strong evidence of a recent downturn in favorable sentiment toward the U.S. among South Koreans, but also evidence of a more recent recovery, and many measures of sentiment toward the U.S. have remained strongly positive throughout the period.

As described in Chapter 1, our analyses relied primarily on data from the U.S. Department of State, which we judged to be the most reliable basis for trend analyses, but we also used data from Gallup Korea, *JoongAng Ilbo*, and other sources to ensure a complete picture.[1]

Attitudes Toward the United States

The U.S. as the Most Liked and Disliked Country

South Korean polling organizations occasionally have asked an open-ended question that asks respondents to volunteer which country they like and dislike the most, responses to which are based upon respondents' recall of recent developments, both favorable and unfavorable, that may have affected South

---

[1]Readers who are interested in the detailed data presented here are encouraged to review Baik and Larson (forthcoming).

Korea.[2] Typically, the U.S. has been among the highest-ranked in both categories.

As shown in Figure 3.1, polling by Gallup Korea suggests that the percentage mentioning the U.S. as the most liked country declined from 19 to 13 percent between late 1994 and February 2002,[3] while polling by *JoongAng Ilbo* shows an increase from about 14 to 19 percent from 1996 to 2001, with the most recent reading, from the September 2003 *JoongAng Ilbo*-CSIS-RAND survey, suggesting that it has remained at that level.

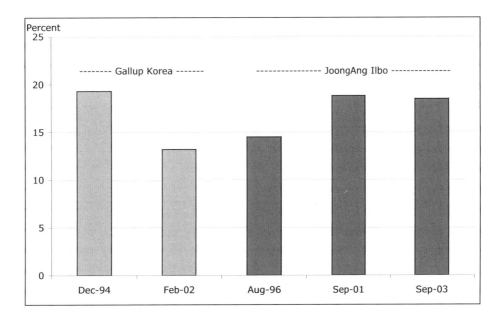

Figure 3.1—Percentage Mentioning U.S. as Most Liked Country[4]

The difference in the trends seems largely attributable to timing: had *JoongAng* asked its question in late February 2002, because of the surge in unfavorable attitudes following the Ohno skating incident (to be discussed in greater detail), it probably would have found far fewer South Koreans mentioning the U.S. as the most liked country.

---

[2]Put another way, an open-ended question such as this elicits responses which, unless a follow-up question is asked, provides little information as to why the respondent likes or dislikes the country s/he names.

[3]As we shall see later, this was a low point in sentiment toward the U.S.

[4]Because of potential differences in sampling frames and other features that may reduce their comparability, these data are presented as two separate time series.

44

The trend data on those mentioning the U.S. as their most disliked country tell a somewhat more sobering story (Figure 3.2).

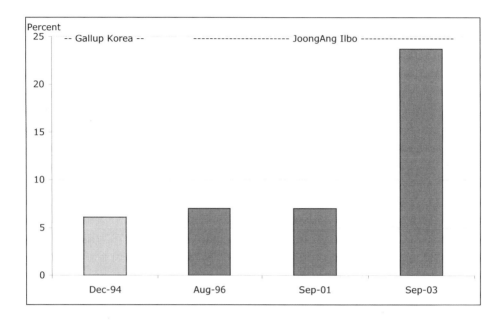

Figure 3.2—Percentage Mentioning U.S. as Most Disliked Country

The Gallup Korea and *JoongAng Ilbo* polling for 1994 through 2001 suggest that only about 6-7 percent were mentioning the U.S. as their most disliked country during much of this period (no data point is available for February 2002). By contrast, the most recent reading from *JoongAng Ilbo* suggests a fairly dramatic increase in unfavorable sentiment toward the U.S.: almost one in four volunteered the U.S. in response to this question, about four times higher than had been measured previously.

Taken together, these results suggest growing ambivalence about the U.S.: there has been something of a recovery in the percentage of those who, when asked which country they like most, think of the U.S., but there also has been an increase in the percentage who think of the U.S. as the most disliked country.

Favorable and Unfavorable Attitudes Toward the U.S.

The U.S. Department of State's Office of Research has, since 1988, frequently surveyed South Koreans on a range of attitudes toward the U.S., U.S.-South

Korean relations, U.S. policy, and other matters.[5] Among the questions they
have asked is whether, overall, respondents have a favorable or unfavorable
opinion of the U.S., and how strongly they feel about that; Gallup Korea, which
conducts the polling for the State Department, also has asked this question on a
number of other occasions, resulting in a fairly comprehensive time series.[6]

Figure 3.3 reports the trend line for the State Department's polling on this
question from 1988 through September 2001,[7] with an additional four data
points from identically worded questions in polling done by Gallup Korea.[8]

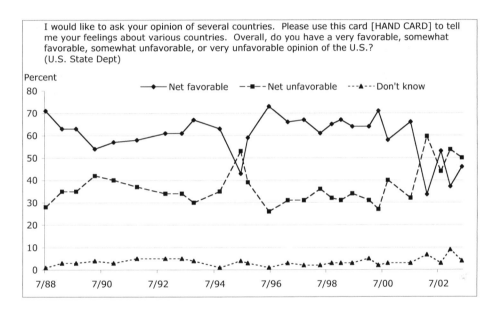

Figure 3.3—Trends in Attitudes Toward the U.S., 1988–2003

As shown in the figure, there have been three periods (June 1995, February 2002,
and December 2002) where attitudes were more unfavorable than favorable:
there was a significant downturn in Koreans' attitudes toward the U.S. in

---

[5]For many years polling was conducted by the United States Information Agency, a now-
defunct independent agency under the policy direction of the U.S. Department of State.

[6]In an ideal world, South Korean polling organizations (or their clients) would have the
resources to ask key questions such as these on a monthly or quarterly basis, which would give
analysts a better basis for correlating changes in attitudes to developments on the ground. The State
Department generally fields polls in South Korea about twice a year.

[7]The data are tabulated in Appendix A.

[8]The Office of Research provided RAND with trend data through July 2001; more recent data
are embargoed, as their policy is to release the data two years after the polling. Gallup Korea asked
the same question in polling that it did for its own purposes, as well as on behalf of the Pew Research
Center. This will be described in greater detail below.

February 2002, even more serious than the previous major downturn in June 1995. After a modest recovery in the summer of 2002, there was another downturn in December 2002, that was attributable to the acquittal of the U.S. soldiers whose armored vehicle killed the vehicle the preceding June, and possibly the election.[9] The most recent data, from May-June 2003—and the September 2003 *JoongAng Ilbo*-CSIS-RAND survey—suggest a partial recovery in favorable sentiment toward the U.S.: 46 percent held favorable views in May, and 50 percent held favorable views in September.[10]

It also is important to note that the recent downturns represented a departure from a generally favorable trend in South Koreans' views toward the U.S. since the early 1990s: from 1990 to 1995, an average of 58 percent held overall favorable views toward the U.S., while the average for the 1996–2001 period was eight points higher, at 65.5 percent; this difference was statistically significant.[11]

Figure 3.4 breaks down overall favorable and unfavorable sentiment into the percentages that held strongly favorable, somewhat favorable, somewhat unfavorable, and strongly unfavorable views of the U.S. In the figure, positive assessments (very/somewhat favorable) are in the top of the chart and above the white band for the "Don't know/Refused to answer" category, and negative assessments (very/somewhat unfavorable) are at the bottom, and below the white band.

As shown in the figure, the percentages holding strong views—whether favorable or unfavorable—typically have been in a distinct minority—5 to 10 percent. By comparison, most South Koreans have tended to place themselves in the middle categories, holding views of the U.S. that are either somewhat favorable or unfavorable.[12]

---

[9]This will be described in more detail in Chapter Four. It also is worth mentioning that we don't know the precise time at which favorable sentiment might have bottomed out; the actual nadirs could have occurred either before or after those shown in the figure. Moreover, it is quite possible that the decline in favorable sentiment in the December 2002 time period actually reached or exceeded the levels eight months earlier—other measures such as the frequency or attendance of demonstrations or candlelight vigils suggest that this could be the case—but if so, it is masked by the vagaries of the timing of the polls. This is one of the difficulties in analyzing the results of polling that is done infrequently.

[10]In addition to the Gallup Korea polling reported in the figure, polling by *Hankook Ilbo* in May 2003 and by *JoongAng Ilbo* in June 2003 showed an improvement over their December 2002 reading of sentiment toward the U.S. See "ROK Daily Polls Public Views on US Relations, ROK President" (2003), and Pu-kun (2003).

[11]A t-test of the difference between these two proportions showed that the difference was statistically significant at the .001 level.

[12]There are a number of possible reasons for this, and they are not mutually exclusive. For example, it could be that because the U.S.-South Korean relationship is so complex, the tendency toward the middle may be because South Koreans are essentially hedging in their judgments, and avoiding either strident or overly exuberant positions. The tendency toward moderation that is a tenet of Confucianism also may play a part. Finally, it may be that the way South Koreans parse the

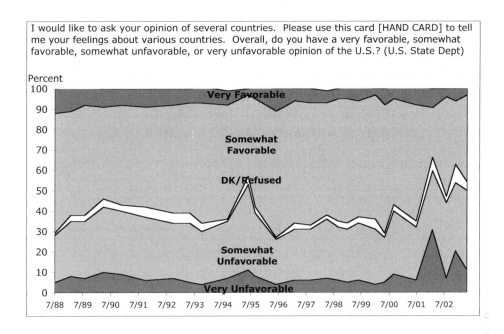

I would like to ask your opinion of several countries. Please use this card [HAND CARD] to tell me your feelings about various countries. Overall, do you have a very favorable, somewhat favorable, somewhat unfavorable, or very unfavorable opinion of the U.S.? (U.S. State Dept)

Figure 3.4—Attitudes Toward the U.S., 1988–2003

These data also enable us to diagnose the various periods in which favorable sentiment declined. For example, during the June 1995 downturn, the growth in unfavorable sentiment was largely attributable to a swelling in the ranks of those who were *somewhat* unfavorable; there was only modest growth in those who held *very* unfavorable views of the U.S.

By comparison, the February 2002 downturn—and to a lesser extent, the December 2002 downturn—resulted from dramatic growth among those holding *very* unfavorable views. What appears to have happened is that perhaps half of those holding moderately favorable views abandoned this position, and swelled the ranks of those holding an unfavorable position.[13] To provide a better sense of the factors that, in combination, seem to have led to these downturns, we will describe the June 1995, February 2002, and December 2002 episodes in more depth in the next chapter.

---

question's wording (in English, it reads as "Regardless of your opinion of the U.S., how would you describe relations between the U.S. and Korea at the present time -- very good, fairly good, fairly poor, or very poor?") leads to a high rate of moderate responses for other reasons.

[13]If support has a graceful failure mode, the movements generally would be dominated by movements from a somewhat favorable view to a somewhat unfavorable view, and from a somewhat unfavorable view to a very unfavorable view. This is, however, pure conjecture, as we don't have panel data that enables us to track individuals' positions over time.

Attitudes Regarding U.S.-South Korean Relations

Another important measure of South Koreans' attitudes toward the U.S. is how they view the state of U.S.-South Korean relations.

The U.S. State Department's trend data on the matter suggests that South Koreans' evaluations of U.S.-South Korean relations have been somewhat more volatile than overall favorable sentiment toward the U.S. (see Figure 3.5), suggesting that these attitudes may be somewhat more responsive to events.[14]

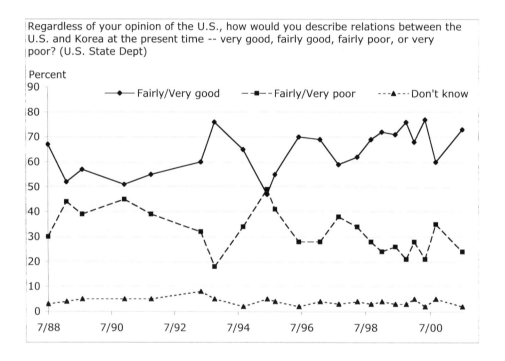

Figure 3.5 –Opinion on the State of U.S.-Korean Relations, 1988–2001

These data—which are only available through July 2001—also show both a significant downturn in Koreans' perceptions of bilateral relations in June 1995, and an overall improvement over the decade: the average percentage saying U.S.-South Korean relations were very or fairly good from 1990 to 1995 was 58.4 percent, while the average for the 1996–2001 period was 68.8 percent; the difference was statistically significant.[15]

---

[14]The standard deviation for overall favorability toward the U.S. was 6.4, whereas that for overall favorable views of the U.S.-South Korean relationship was 8.8. Volatility in South Korean attitudes also can be found in Koreans' commitment to democracy, which fluctuates in response to various political and economic forces. See Shin, Park, and Jang (2002), pp. 23–24.

[15]A t-test of the difference between these proportions was significant at the .001 level.

When these data are broken out by strength of feeling on the matter (Figure 3.6), we again see that those who think that U.S.-South Korean relations are very good are typically only a minority of 5-10 percent, and those who think U.S.-South Korean relations are very bad typically comprise 5 percent or fewer of those polled. And again, most of the movement in the percentage unfavorable appears to be attributable to movements from "fairly good" to "fairly poor." On only one occasion—during the June 1995 downturn—did more South Koreans have an unfavorable than favorable view of the bilateral relationship.

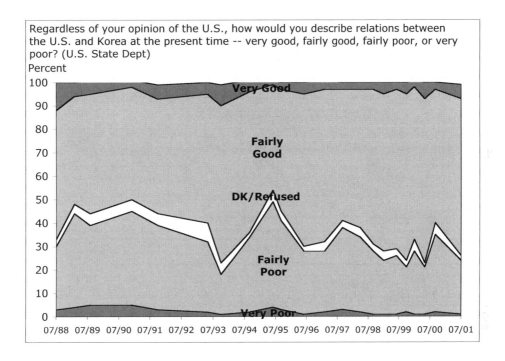

Figure 3.6—Opinion on the State of U.S.-Korean Relations, 1988–2001

Because our time series data from the State Department end in September 2001, we compare these data with more recent polling from another source: the September 2003 *JoongAng Ilbo*-CSIS-RAND poll. That poll had a much less favorable result: nearly one in three (32.5 percent) said that the relationship at that time either was very good (1.6 percent) or pretty good (30.9 percent), whereas 66.4 percent characterized the relationship either as pretty bad (61.0 percent) or very bad (5.4 percent).[16]

---

[16] *JoongAng Ilbo*CSIS-RAND, September 15–17, 2003, N=1,000.

Attitudes Regarding Americans

Another important measure of South Korean attitudes toward things American is their attitudes toward Americans themselves, and comparisons of how these attitudes differ with attitudes toward the U.S. According to the available data, majorities of South Koreans typically held more favorable views of Americans than the U.S. during the recent downturn.

Table 3.1 presents data on the percentages who held a favorable opinion of the U.S. and Americans in two polls conducted by the Pew Research Center and Gallup Korea in August 2002 and May 2003; a positive difference ("+") connotes a higher percentage having favorable attitudes toward Americans than for the U.S. Although the size of this difference depends greatly on which poll we look at, the results suggest that most South Koreans consistently have held favorable attitudes toward Americans, more favorable than those toward the U.S. as a whole.

Table 3.1

Comparison of South Korean Attitudes Toward the U.S. and Americans

Please tell me if you have a very favorable, somewhat favorable, somewhat unfavorable or very unfavorable opinion of…the United States

Please tell me if you have a very favorable, somewhat favorable, somewhat unfavorable or very unfavorable opinion of…Americans

AUGUST 2002

	U.S.	Americans	Difference
Very favorable	4	4	0
Somewhat favorable	49	57	+8
Somewhat unfavorable	37	30	−7
Very unfavorable	7	5	−2
Don't know/Refused	3	4	+1

MAY 2003

	U.S.	Americans	Difference
Very favorable	3	4	+1
Somewhat favorable	43	70	+27
Somewhat unfavorable	39	17	−22
Very unfavorable	11	3	−8
Don't know/Refused	4	7	+3

SOURCE: Pew Research Center/Gallup Korea, 2002 Global Attitudes Survey, August 2002 and May 2003.

Attitudes Regarding the Alliance and the U.S. Military Presence

In contrast to the attitudes toward the U.S., which were shown to exhibit substantial volatility, large majorities of South Koreans have consistently favored the bilateral alliance, have believed U.S. forces are important to their security, and have favored U.S. forces remaining in South Korea for five or more years.

The U.S.-ROK Alliance

The available data for 1997–2001 suggest that 60 percent or more South Koreans consistently have indicated that Korea should maintain its alliance with the U.S. even after reunification of the peninsula, while a minority of 30–35 percent have suggested the alliance will no longer be needed at that time (Figure 3.7).

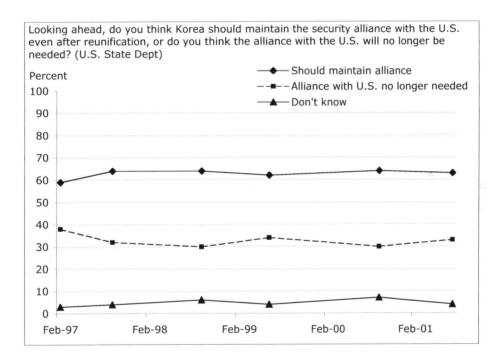

Figure 3.7—Attitudes Toward Maintaining the Alliance After Reunification, 1997–2001

This is among the most stable attitudes we have thus far presented.[17] Although we lack true time series data for the most recent period, the available data

---

[17]The percentage who said that the alliance should be maintained after reunification ranged from 59 to 64 percent.

suggest that favorable views of the alliance may have been affected in the December 2002-February 2003 downturn, but otherwise they have held up well.

Polling by *Hankook Ilbo* in May 2002 and May 2003 found a consistent majority with favorable attitudes of the alliance. Polling in May 2002 found that a modest majority—56.4 percent of those polled in May 200—thought that South Korea should intensify the alliance (6.3 percent) or maintain friendly relations (50.1 percent), whereas 31.8 percent thought South Korea should outgrow U.S.-centered diplomacy, and 10.3 percent thought South Korea should keep its distance from the U.S.[18] Polling one year later showed much more favorable attitudes: 76.3 percent thought that South Korea should intensify the alliance (17.8 percent) or maintain friendly relations (58.5 percent), whereas 23 percent thought South Korea should outgrow U.S. –centered diplomacy (18.2 percent) or keep its distance from the U.S. (4.8 percent).[19]

On the other hand, *JoongAng Ilbo's* January 2003 poll—taken during the downturn that began in late November 2002—found only 40 percent in favor of restoring the traditional alliance between the U.S. and South Korea (33 percent) or cooperating with the U.S. in a U.S.-led world order (7 percent), while 48 percent supported outgrowing the policies centering on the U.S., and 12 percent favored review of all diplomatic and security policies centering on the U.S. (11.8 percent).[20]

Finally, the September 2003 *JoongAng Ilbo*-CSIS-RAND survey asked those who thought reunification was possible (62 percent) if they supported maintaining the alliance after reunification. Although the difference probably is attributable to question structure and wording, and understates support for the alliance, the result was much lower support for maintaining the alliance: 33.3 percent thought the alliance should be maintained after reunification, while 28.7 percent did not; we conjecture that many of the 36.5 percent who felt that there was no possibility

---

[18]*Hankook Ilbo* and Media Research, May 27, 2002, N=1,000. The question that was asked on both occasions was: "Which of the following phrases comes closer to your opinion on our relations with the United States: We should intensify the alliance with the US; We should maintain friendly relations with the US; We should outgrow the US-centered diplomacy; We should keep our distance away from the US as much as possible."

[19]*Hankook Ilbo*, May 28, 2003, N=1,000.

[20]*JoongAng Ilbo*, January 413, 2003, N=1,200. JoongAng Ilbo asked: "Which of the following phrases comes closer to your opinion of a desirable relationship between the US and South Korea? We should review all of the diplomatic and security policies centering around the US; We should outgrow the policies centering around the US; We should restore the traditional alliance with the US; We should cooperate with the US in the US-led maintaining of world order."

for reunification with the north most likely also favored continuation of the alliance.[21]

Attitudes Toward the Importance of U.S. Military Forces

Even larger percentages of South Koreans—typically more than three out of four —have indicated their belief that U.S. military forces are very or somewhat important to protecting Korea's security (Figure 3.8), than approved of continuation of the alliance after reunification. And although the data are somewhat spotty, these beliefs seem to have held up in the most recent period.

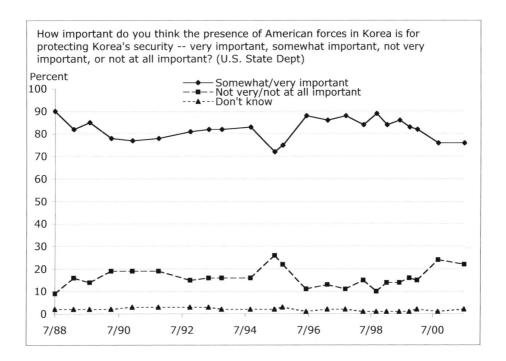

Figure 3.8—Importance of American Forces for Protecting Korea's Security, 1988–2001

As with some of the other measures reported earlier, on average, South Koreans during the 1996–2001 period exhibited more favorable beliefs than in the earlier 1990–1995 period: The percentage saying that U.S. forces were very or somewhat important for protecting South Korea's security averaged 79 percent for the 1990–1995 period and 83.8 percent for the 1996–2001 period, a statistically

---

[21]Their preferences regarding maintaining the alliance were not reported; the question was asked only of those who thought reunification was possible.

significant difference.[22] Nevertheless, a downward trend also is evident in the 1998–2001 period.[23]

When broken out by strength of feeling (Figure 3.9), we see that the percentage who think that U.S. forces are not at all important is a very small share of the total—less than 5 percent—whereas those who think that U.S. forces are very important ranges from about 20 to nearly 50 percent and those thinking they are somewhat important account for 40–50 percent. Again, we can see a downturn in attitudes toward the importance of U.S. forces in June 1995, and some erosion in beliefs about the importance of U.S. forces over 1998–2001.

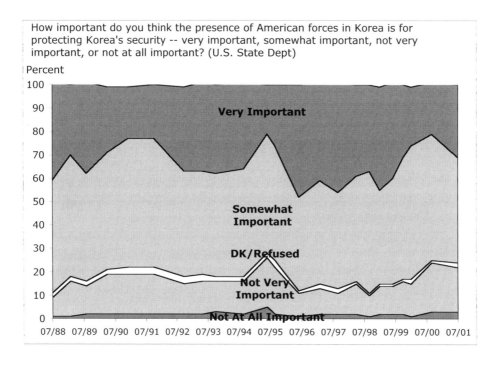

Figure 3.9—Importance of American Forces for Protecting Korea's Security, 1988–2001

Although we know very little about attitudes in the intervening periods, the belief that U.S. forces were important more or less weathered the most recent downturn: polling by *The Hankyoreh* showed a decline from 72 percent in June 2000 (at the time of the summit) to a modest majority of about 58 percent in March 2002 (after the skating incident) in those saying that it was necessary for

---

[22]A t-test of the difference between these proportions was significant at the .001 level.

[23]As was described in Chapter 2, two reasonable conjectures are growing optimism about the prospects for reunification that were reflected in then-President Kim Dae Jung's "Sunshine Policy," and declining perceptions of the threat from the north. We later present some evidence on this issue.

U.S. forces to be stationed in South Korea.[24] This suggests that the majority belief in the importance of U.S. forces may have held through the February 2002 downturn.

And polling by Gallup Korea in July 2003 suggests there was a modest increase in South Koreans' estimation of the importance of U.S. forces since July 2001: the percentage saying U.S. forces were very or somewhat important to South Korea's security rose from 76 percent in July 2001 to 82 percent in July 2003;[25] and the September 2003 *JoongAng Ilbo*-CSIS-RAND survey showed 87.3 percent who believed that U.S. forces were very or somewhat important to South Korea's security.

Attitudes Toward the Withdrawal of U.S. Forces

The State Department's trend data on attitudes toward the withdrawal of U.S. forces (see Figure 3.10) only covers the 1988–1996 period, but these data suggest that only a small percentage of South Koreans—no more than three in ten—think that U.S. forces should withdraw immediately or in the immediate future of the next two or three years. By comparison, about seven in ten appear to believe that U.S. forces should remain longer, five years or more. Although a downturn also is apparent in the more recent period, favorable attitudes toward the continued presence of U.S. forces also appear to have held up reasonably well.

Although the question is worded in a way that provides less insight into South Koreans' attitudes on the matter, *JoongAng Ilbo's* polling record also provides a reasonably good trend on the question of withdrawal (Figure 3.11); these data suggest a downturn in support for the U.S. presence in mid-December 2002 but a recovery by June 2003, at which time 60 percent thought that U.S. forces should remain stationed (29 percent) or be stationed for a while (31 percent), and 40 percent felt otherwise.[26]

By contrast, Gallup Korea's mid-December 2002 question found only 32 percent who approved of withdrawing U.S. forces at the time,[27] and *JoongAng Ilbo's* mid-

---

[24]*The Hankyoreh*, June 26, 200, N=700 and March 8-9/2002, N=500.

[25]Gallup Korea asked the State Department's question again in their polling of July 1–10, 2003.

[26]*JoongAng Ilbo*, June 9-10, 2003, N=1,032.

[27]Gallup Korea asked "Do you think U.S. military forces in South Korea should be withdrawn? Or do you think they should be stationed?" Gallup Korea, December 14, 2002, N=1,054. An earlier polling result was not available for comparison.

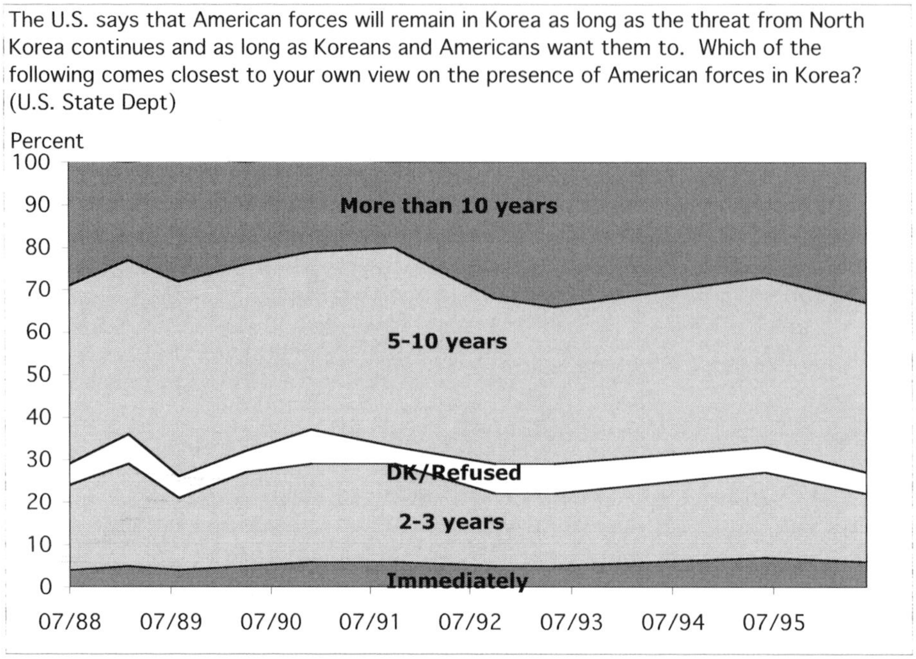

The U.S. says that American forces will remain in Korea as long as the threat from North Korea continues and as long as Koreans and Americans want them to. Which of the following comes closest to your own view on the presence of American forces in Korea? (U.S. State Dept)
Percent
100
90
80
70
60
50
40
30
20
10
0
More than 10 years
5-10 years
DK/Refused
2-3 years
Immediately
07/88
07/89
07/90
07/91
07/92
07/93
07/94
07/95

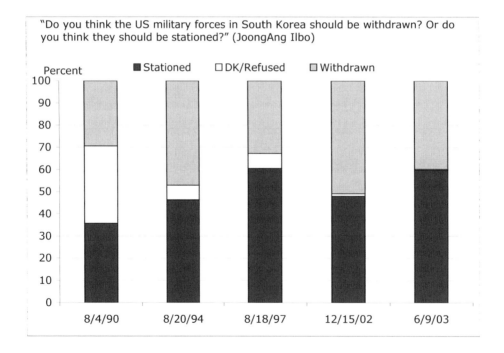

Figure 3.10—Attitudes Toward a U.S. Withdrawal, 1988–1996

"Do you think the US military forces in South Korea should be withdrawn? Or do you think they should be stationed?" (JoongAng Ilbo)
Percent
Stationed
DK/Refused
Withdrawn
100
90
80
70
60
50
40
30
20
10
0
8/4/90
8/20/94
8/18/97
12/15/02
6/9/03

Figure 3.11—Attitudes Toward a U.S. Withdrawal, 1990–2003

December poll found only 6.3 percent who said U.S. forces should be withdrawn immediately and another 44.6 who said they should be withdrawn gradually.[28]

Finally, *JoongAng Ilbo's* polling in February 2003 found only 14 percent who thought that U.S. force should be withdrawn completely or largely reduced,[29] and *The Hankyoreh's* March 2002 polling found 72 percent who said that the withdrawal of U.S. forces should be gradual, and according to the pace of improvement in inter-Korean relations.[30] This suggests that opinion on the matter tends to be highly sensitive to question wording and, especially, perceived progress on inter-Korean relations and reunification.

It also is worth mentioning one result from polling done by *The Hankyoreh* in March 2002. South Koreans were evenly divided on how their government should react to a hypothetical U.S. decision to withdraw U.S. military forces from Korea: 47 percent thought that the ROK government should try to dissuade the U.S. in such an instance, whereas 46 percent thought it should not.[31]

As shown in Figure 3.11, when respondents were given only two crude options the result is somewhat greater volatility, with three of the polls (in 1990, 1994, and 2002) showing less than a majority preferring that U.S. forces continue to be stationed in South Korea,[32] and two (in 1997 and June 2003) showing six in ten favoring the continued stationing of U.S. forces. And as described above, of the roughly 50 percent who told the *JoongAng Ilbo's* mid-December poll that U.S. forces should be withdrawn, only 6.3 percent said that U.S. forces should be withdrawn immediately, while the remaining 44.6 said they should be withdrawn "gradually"—not a particularly alarming finding.

The September 2003 *JoongAng Ilbo*-CSIS-RAND survey also included a question asking respondents whether they favored U.S. forces immediately withdrawing, withdrawing soon, staying "for a decent amount of time," or staying even after reunification. Only 26.6 percent preferred the two most-immediate-withdrawal options, while 73 percent preferred the options that would have U.S. forces stay much longer.[33] Taken together, and despite the volatility in the *JoongAng* series,

---

[28]*JoongAng Ilbo*, December 19, 2002, N=1,030.

[29]*JoongAng Ilbo*, February 12, 2003, N=1,200.

[30]*The Hankyoreh*, March 8–9, 2002, N=500.

[31]*The Hankyoreh*, March 12, 2002, N=500.

[32]It also is notable that the 1990 result had an unduly large percentage of South Koreans who were undecided on the matter.

[33]Four percent favored immediate withdrawal, 22.4 percent favored withdrawal soon, 62.9 percent preferred staying "for a decent amount of time," and 10.1 percent preferred staying even after reunification. *JoongAng Ilbo*-CSIS-RAND survey, September 15–17, 2001, N=1,000.

one again gets the sense that a majority of South Koreans continued to favor the continued presence of U.S. forces in the near- and mid-term.

This support, however, masks a deep ambivalence about the presence of U.S. forces. On the one hand, most South Koreans have said that U.S. forces are important to their security, but on the other, they believe that the presence of U.S. forces may impede the pace of reunification or adversely affect other goals.[34] Thus, before moving on, it is worth noting South Koreans' responses to questions that have asked *why* they favor or oppose the stationing of U.S. forces in Korea (see Tables 3.2 and 3.3).

Table 3.2

Reasons For and Against U.S. Military Forces in South Korea, June 2000

"Why do you think it is necessary for the US military forces to be stationed in South Korea?"*

Opinion	Percent
To prevent North Korea from invading South Korea	65.3%
To prevent Japan from rearmament	12.5
To keep China in check	9.4
Others / Don't know / Refused	12.8

"Why do you think it is unnecessary for the US military forces to be stationed in South Korea?"**

Opinion	Percent
For the autonomous reunification of Korea	55.6%
To improve the inter-Korean relations and reunify the Korean peninsula	13.9
To conclude a peace agreement between South and North Korea	11.7
Others / Don't know / Refused	18.8

Source: *The Hankyoreh 21*, 7/18/00, polling on 06/26/00, Adults aged 20 & older, n=700.
Notes: * = Asked of the 71.7 percent who said it was necessary for the US military forces to be stationed in South Korea; ** = Asked of the 25.7 percent who said it was unnecessary for the US military forces to be stationed in South Korea.

Among those who think U.S. forces are unnecessary, a plurality typically have suggested that the presence of U.S. forces complicates reunification and improved relations with the north, although some have cited the desire for military self-reliance, or expressed the belief that there no longer is any threat from the north and that U.S. forces are therefore unnecessary.

---

[34]For example, polling by *The Hankyoreh* in September 2000 found that 71 percent of those polled felt that it was necessary to station U.S. military forces in South Korea, and 62 percent felt that this presence could be an obstacle to the progress of the inter-Korean relationship. *The Hankyoreh*, September 16–17, 2000, N=1,000.

The dominant reason given by those favoring the continued stationing of U.S. forces—mentioned by about two out of three of these respondents—has been to prevent North Korean aggression. Other reasons also have been offered, however, ranging from checking potential threats from Japan and China to simply maintaining friendly relations with the U.S.

Table 3.3

Reasons For and Against U.S. Military Forces in South Korea, March 2002

"Why do you think it is necessary for the US military forces to be stationed in South Korea?"*

Opinion	Percent
To prevent North Korea from invading South Korea	60.1%
To maintain friendly relations with the US	24.6
To prevent Japan from rearmament	3.8
To prevent South Korea from invading North Korea	1.2
To keep China in check	1.4
Others/Don't know/Refused (DK/Refused = 3.0)	8.9

"Why do you think it is unnecessary for the US military forces to be stationed in South Korea?"**

Opinion	Percent
To improve the inter-Korean relations and reunify the Korean peninsula	38.7%
To protect the human and civil rights of South Koreans	24.3
For the military autonomy of South Korea	24.5
The risk of war brought on by North Korea has disappeared	7.6
Others/Don't know/Refused (DK/Refused = 3.0)	5.0

Source: *The Hankyoreh 21*, March 12, 2002, based on polling done 3/8-9/02, Adults aged 20 & older, n=500
Notes: * = Asked of the 57.7 percent who said it is necessary for the US military forces to be stationed in South Korea; ** = Asked of the 33.4 percent who said it is unnecessary for US military forces to be stationed in South Korea.

How Do South Koreans' Attitudes Toward the U.S. Compare With Those Toward Other Nations?

Of course, South Korean attitudes toward the U.S. also can be assessed in a comparative framework. One frame of reference is a comparison between South Koreans' attitudes toward the U.S. and their attitudes toward other nations.

Best Descriptions of Other Nations

Of interest is how South Koreans' overall impressions of the U.S. compare with their impressions of Japan and China.[35] Table 3.4 presents data from November 1999 on which of eight descriptors South Koreans chose to describe the U.S., China, and Japan. (Note that the data are several years old and much has happened since 1999).

Table 3.4

Koreans' Views on Best Descriptions of U.S., Japan, and China, November 1999

Which of these statements BEST describes…the United States…Japan…China

	U.S.	Japan	China
Major economic power	34	42	3
Democratic state	29	2	1
The financial situation is the highest priority	16	35	6
The society too divided by rich and poor	10	2	15
Egalitarian society	6	2	3
Major military power	5	1	16
Has a unique culture and tradition	1	10	38
Strongly bureaucratic society	*	2	17
Don't know	*	1	*

Source: Taylor (1999), available at http://www.harrisinteractive.com/harris_poll/.
Note: * = Less than 1 percent.

South Koreans seem to have a fairly discriminating view of the characteristics of each of the three countries. Whereas nearly eight in ten thought of the U.S. either as a major economic power, a democratic state, or a nation where the financial situation was the highest priority, comparable percentages thought of China as having a unique culture and tradition, a strongly bureaucratic society, or as a major military power, and thought of Japan as a major economic power or a country where the financial situation received the highest priority. By comparison, where only about 5 percent thought of the U.S. as a major military power or an egalitarian society, more than 15 percent described China this way. And 10 percent thought of the U.S. as a society that was too divided by rich and poor, which was smaller than the percentage that used that phrase to describe China.

The impression one gets from these data is that although South Koreans have very different impressions of the three countries, their views of other nations

_____

[35]Comparable data were not available on North Korea or Russia.

tend to be dominated by just a few key characteristics.[36] It also is worth pointing out that the U.S. appears to fare well in most of these comparisons.

Most Liked and Disliked Countries

Another point of comparison is the frequency with which South Koreans mention different countries as the most liked or disliked countries when presented with an open-ended question (see Table 3.5).

Table 3.5

Countries Most Liked by South Koreans, 1994–2003

	Gallup Korea	JoongAng Ilbo*	Joongang Ilbo	Gallup Korea	JoongAng Ilbo-CSIS-RAND
	12/94	8/96	9/01	2/02	9/03
United States	19.3	14.5	18.8	13.2	18.5
Australia	10.3	13.1	18.9	14.2	10.2
Switzerland	13.6	15.1	10.6	7.6	7.7
Canada	2.4		12.3		6.9
France	5.3		4.2		4.7
China				6.6	
Japan				6.2	
Others		41.1			

NOTE: *The August 1996 *JoongAng Ilbo* poll reported only four countries and, unlike the other polls, it reported the percentage mentioning South Korea (16.2 percent—part of the "Others" category); the other polls evidently did not allow respondents to mention their own country. Missing data are attributable to the fact that not all sources reported all responses. For details of question wording and other features, see Baik and Eric Larson (forthcoming). *[Can't cite this reference]*

As shown in the table, the U.S. has been among South Koreans' favorites, typically either in the first or second position in competition with Australia or Switzerland, and mentioned by anywhere from 13 to 19 percent of respondents.

Table 3.6 reports the countries South Koreans most often mentioned as the most *disliked* ones; again, the U.S. is prominent, even if not the most disliked nation. In fact, the most recent reading on the matter—from the September 2003 *JoongAng Ilbo*-CSIS-RAND poll—shows nearly twice as many South Koreans identifying the U.S. as North Korea, and nearly as many mentioning the U.S. as mentioned Japan. Particularly significant—and worrisome—is the more frequent naming of the U.S. (mentioned by nearly one in four respondents) as compared with North

---

[36]Of course, an open-ended question might result in a richer set of characterizations of each nation.

Korea (mentioned by fewer than one in seven), and the fact that fewer mention the U.S. as the country they like most (less than one in five) than as the country they like least (one in four). This suggests that, even in spite of recent efforts by U.S. and South Korean leaders to foster more favorable public attitudes toward the U.S., the ranks of those who express the strongest negative feelings about the U.S.—as measured by their response to an open-ended question by mentioning the U.S.—have swelled recently.

Table 3.6

Countries Most Disliked by South Koreans, 1994–2003

	Gallup Korea	JoongAng Ilbo*	Joongang Ilbo	JoongAng Ilbo-CSIS
	12/94	8/96	9/01	9/03
Japan	47.6	51.4	63.4	25.6
North Korea	16.8	22.3	10.8	12.7
U.S.	6.1	7.0	7.0	23.7
Russia	2.1		0.8	
Switzerland		3.9		
Australia		2.4		
China			2.8	

NOTE: For details of question wording and other features, see Baik and Larson (forthcoming).

The impression one gets from these data—which is consistent with much of the other data presented above—is that a minority of South Koreans tend to think of the U.S. when asked to name the country that elicits the strongest feelings, whether favorable or unfavorable, and that the size of this group fluctuates somewhat over time in response to a variety of influences. It also provides additional evidence that, as of September 2003, a full recovery in favorable sentiment toward the U.S. had yet to take place.

Favorable and Unfavorable Sentiment Toward Other Nations

We can also compare our measure of the *strength* of favorable and unfavorable sentiment toward the U.S. with that toward several other nations. Figure 3.12 compares favorable attitudes toward the U.S. with other data from the State Department on South Koreans' sentiment toward these other countries.[37]

---

[37]The question was the same as that used for the U.S. and reported earlier: "I would like to ask your opinion of several countries. Please use this card [HAND CARD] to tell me your feelings about various countries. Overall, do you have a very favorable, somewhat favorable, somewhat unfavorable, or very unfavorable opinion of [COUNTRY]?"

As shown in the figure, where more South Koreans held favorable attitudes toward the U.S. than toward China from 1988 to 1994, net favorable sentiment toward China has since caught up with—and on a number of occasions, even surpassed—that for the U.S. Indeed, in July 2001, 73 percent of those polled had favorable attitudes toward China, whereas only 66 percent held favorable views of the U.S. In a similar vein, net favorable sentiment toward Japan also has increased since about 1995, and stood at around four in ten in July 2001, much lower than that for the U.S. to be sure, but a significant increase nonetheless.

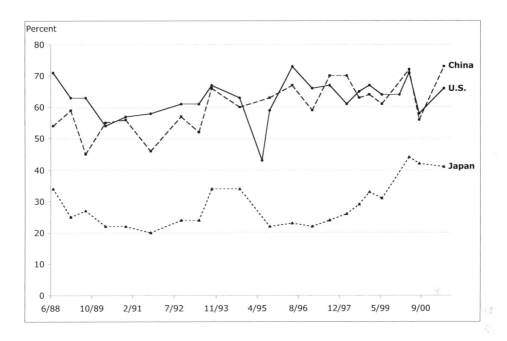

Figure 3.12—Favorable Sentiment Toward the U.S., China, and Japan, 1988–2001

Less obviously, there appears to be somewhat more volatility in South Koreans' attitudes toward China and Japan than toward the U.S.;[38] the reason may well be that attitudes toward these nations are not constrained by the stabilizing influence of the U.S.-South Korean security relationship, which, as we shall see, seems to help dampen wider swings in sentiment toward the U.S.[39]

Although it is not yet clear whether these trends will continue, they most certainly bear watching. One possibility is that China's growing economic importance to South Korea and its increasingly important role in influencing North Korean behavior could well portend more favorable attitudes toward

---

[38]The standard deviation for the data on favorability toward the U.S. was 4.9, while the standard deviations in the data for China and Japan were 7.8 and 7.2, respectively.

[39]We will present evidence in support of this conjecture in the next section.

China, possibly even at the expense of attitudes toward the U.S.[40] Japan, long viewed as an enemy by many South Koreans, increasingly tends to be seen benignly, and many younger Koreans find much to be admired in Japan.[41]

Chapter Conclusions

This chapter has provided a *tour d'horizon* of trends in a wide range of attitudes toward the U.S. As discussed in this chapter, the data suggested rather marked declines in favorable sentiment toward the U.S. in February 2002 and then again in December 2002 that rivaled or surpassed the earlier downturn in June 1995. The February 2002 downturn occurred about a month after President Bush's "axis of evil" speech and at the time of the Ohno skating incident; the December 2002 downturn followed the trial that acquitted the U.S. soldiers whose armored vehicle killed two schoolgirls, and happened at the time of the December 2002 South Korean presidential elections. While it is certainly possible that the decline in favorable public sentiment in December 2002—at least as measured by the available public opinion data—might have reached (or even surpassed) the low set ten months earlier, the February 2002 reading by Gallup Korea remains the lowest measured point, according to the available data.[42] Taken together, these data are consistent with the explanation that the recent broad-based downturn in favorable attitudes toward the U.S. was primarily an emotional—or as some Korean observers put it, "sentimental"—reaction to a number of high-profile stressors in the relationship.

As was described, some measures—the frequency with which the U.S. is mentioned as the most disliked country, favorable and unfavorable attitudes toward the U.S., and opinions on the health of the U.S.-South Korean relationship—showed a marked decline sometime after 2001, while other opinions—favorable sentiment toward Americans, and the importance of the alliance and U.S. forces—appear to have held up fairly well. Moreover, while there appears to have been at least a partial recovery in overall favorable sentiment toward the U.S. since December 2002, as of the September 2003

---

[40]For example, William Watts' survey of 51 future South Korean opinion leaders aged 30-49 found a majority of 53 percent saying they thought that Korea's ties with China would be more important than its ties with the U.S. in ten years. See Watts (2002), pp. 15–17.

[41]We are indebted to William Watts for this point, who also notes that Russia and, to a lesser extent North Korea also are viewed more benignly, whereas the U.S. comes off in a considerably less charitable light, because U.S. policy often is perceived to be arrogant, self-serving, and destructive of possibilities of North-South dialogue and cooperation.

[42] The frequency and scale of the demonstrations and candlelight vigils in the December 2002-January 2003 period appeared to be much larger than the demonstrations that were held after the Ohno incident for example.

JoongAng Ilbo-CSIS poll that was developed in cooperation with the RAND Corporation, only about one in three thought that the bilateral relationship was in particularly good shape.

As we will describe in the next chapter, the prevalence of this belief may help to account for the fact that there has been only a partial recovery in favorable sentiment toward the U.S. But at an even deeper level, a core set of individual-level beliefs and characteristics and structural sources may also be influencing South Koreans' favorable and unfavorable sentiment toward the U.S. This is the subject of the next chapter.

4. The Sources of South Korean Attitudes Toward the U.S.

In this chapter, we undertake a more systematic and quantitative exploration of the sources of Korean attitudes toward the U.S. and the trends in those attitudes, through a further examination of the available public opinion data on the matter.

We begin the chapter by showing that South Koreans hold somewhat differentiated views of both the U.S. and where problems in the U.S.-South Korean relationship are to be found. To make sense of the various factors identified in Chapters 2 and 3, and to frame the issue in a more policy-relevant way, we then present the results of our statistical modeling, which predicts, with a high degree of accuracy, favorable and unfavorable sentiment based upon a small set of key attitudes and individual-level characteristics. We next discuss some of the individual-level characteristics and attitudes that help to explain South Koreans' attitudes toward the U.S., and can serve as lenses that bias attitudes toward the U.S. in one direction or another. Finally, we discuss some societal factors that also may be influencing South Koreans' views of the U.S.

Many Views of the U.S. and of Where the Problems Lie

When asked to choose from a list of descriptors the one that best describes the U.S., South Koreans offer a variety of opinions on the most distinctive feature of the United States.[1] As shown in Table 4.1:

- About a third think of the U.S. as a major economic power, about the same percentage as American respondents.

- Nearly as many South Koreans think of the U.S. as a democratic state, which is about twice the percentage of Americans who chose this description.

- Sixteen percent of Koreans think of the U.S. as a nation in which financial issues are given the highest priority, more than twice the percentage of Americans who think of the U.S. this way.

---

[1] South Koreans' views of the U.S. were compared with those toward China and Japan in the previous chapter.

- Ten percent of Koreans (and Americans as well) see U.S. society as too divided on the basis of wealth, while 6 percent of Koreans think of the U.S. as an egalitarian society (more than the Americans).

- Somewhat surprisingly, only 5 percent of Koreans, but fully 21 percent of Americans, think of the U.S. as a major military power.[2]

Table 4.1

Koreans and Americans Views of Statements Best Describing the U.S., November 1999

Which of these statements BEST describes...the United States	Korean Respondents	American Respondents
Major economic power	34%	33%
Democratic state	29	15
The financial situation is the highest priority	16	7
The society too divided by rich and poor	10	10
Egalitarian society	6	1
Major military power	5	21
Has a unique culture and tradition	1	1
Strongly bureaucratic society	*	6
Don't know	*	6

Source: Humphrey Taylor, "Attitudes to United States, Japan and China in U.S. and Seven Asian Countries, The Harris Poll #66, November 10, 1999, available at http://www.harrisinteractive.com/ harris_poll/.

Note: * = Less than 1 percent.

In many ways, then, South Koreans view the U.S. in much the same way Americans view it; where they differ, the data do not suggest that Korean judgments are any harsher than American ones.

South Koreans also have differentiated explanations for frictions in the U.S.-South Korean relationship, and these explanations have shifted over time. Table 4.2 presents the results of polling done by the U.S. State Department in January and September 2000, and shows that the frequency with which different problems are mentioned as the most important ones can vary greatly, with trade frictions to issues of sovereignty and independence, and the historical residue of past incidents and policy differences all being mentioned by some.

As we described in Chapter 2, in many cases, outbreaks of anti-American sentiment can be tied to specific issues or developments. Table 4.3 presents data from a question asked by the *Sisa Journal* in February 2002 (the lowest point in

---

[2]To be clear, many Americans view U.S. military power as a source of national pride, whereas we would expect many or most South Koreans to view it as a negative.

favorable sentiment in our time series data), which sought to understand the reasons some respondents had a worsening impression of the U.S. at that time.

Table 4.2

Biggest Problems in U.S.-South Korean Relations, January and September 2000

What do you see as the biggest problem in relations with the U.S. at present? [OPEN END]

	Jan-00	Sep-00
Friction over trade and economic issues/ market opening pressures	36%	16%
U.S. bullying/sacrifices Korean interests/ forcing Korea to do its will	21	13
U.S. lacks respect for Korea as an equal	6	4
Presence of U.S. troops/bases in Korea	5	16
USFK Status of Forces (SOFA) issues	5	13
Nogun-ri and other Korean war-related incidents	4	--
U.S. handling of talks with North Korea	4	2
Use of Agent Orange/defoliants in Vietnam and in DMZ	2	--
Dispute over South Korean missile range/capability	1	0
U.S. a threat to Korean culture	1	--
Other	0	5
No major problems	5	4
Don't know	10	27
Total	100%	100%

Source: Office of Research, U.S. Department of State.

As shown in the table, nearly two-thirds mentioned the then-fresh incident involving U.S. and South Korean skaters at the Olympics, in which an Olympic referee stripped the Korean skater of the gold medal, and gave it to the American, whereas fewer than one in five mentioned President Bush's "axis of evil" speech,[3] and fewer than 10 percent mentioned U.S. military operations in Afghanistan. The data suggest that the skating incident touched a deep nerve for many Koreans and seems to have gone to the heart both of Koreans' competitive nationalistic instincts and of their sense of fairness. In the minds of most Koreans, Korea was unfairly stripped of a medal that it had rightly won.[4]

---

[3]The available public opinion data on the matter suggests that perhaps two out of three South Koreans felt that the speech was "inappropriate," however.

[4]Sadly, no questions were asked that would have enabled respondents to volunteer reasons for having a less favorable impression of the U.S.; the responses to such a question would have avoided possible bias arising from the specific options presented in this question.

Table 4.3

Reasons for Having a Less Favorable Impression of the United States, February 2002

"Has your impression of the United States changed? If so, is it more favorable or unfavorable, compared to the past?" (Media Research, 02/23/02, Adults aged 20 and older, n=1,013)

Percent Opinion
56.1 Percent saying more unfavorable
43.9 Others / Don't know / Refused

"If your impression of the United States has been getting worse, which of following events is the biggest reason? (Media research, 02/23/02, Adults aged 20 & older, n=1,013)

Percent	Opinion
65.0	Referee's judgment of the short-track games at Salt Lake City Winter Olympic Games
18.8	President Bush's speech on 'axis of evil'
8.1	The US war against Afghanistan
3.5	Discharge of toxic chemicals from the US military base
3.0	Apartment construction for American soldiers in the U.S. military base at Yongsan
0.7	Pressure to open the agricultural market
0.7	Pressure to buy F-15 fighter jets
0.2	Crimes committed by American soldiers

Note: This question was asked of the 56.1 percent who said they have more unfavorable impression of the US, comparing to the past.
Source: *Sisa Journal*, 03/07/2002

When asked why some people dislike the U.S. (Table 4.4), those polled again offered a host of explanations, but emphasized a lack of consideration in the bilateral relationship, encroachments on nationalism and sovereignty, some measure of insecurity and envy, and militarism in U.S. policy.[5]

The September 2003 *JoongAng Ilbo*-CSIS-RAND survey also sheds some light on the reasons for unfavorable sentiment. As shown in Table 4.5, most of the reasons respondents cited for people disliking the U.S. had to do with a perceived lack of respect for Korean interests and sovereignty, and for Koreans themselves.

---

[5]Unfortunately, the question did not ask explicitly about the deaths of the schoolgirls the month before. However, the small percentages selecting the presence of U.S. troops suggests that it was not a particularly salient issue yet, and the small percentages selecting "None of these" or "Don't know" suggests that the question did not fundamentally miss its mark in allowing respondents to register the principal reasons for their complaints.

Table 4.4

Main Reasons Some People Dislike the U.S., July 2002

Regardless of how you yourself feel about the U.S., using this card [HAND CARD] what do you think are the main reasons why some people dislike the U.S.? Please look over all the items on this card before telling me which you think are the main reasons why some people dislike the U.S. Any other? [ACCEPT UP TO TWO RESPONSES]

	1st	2nd	Combined
U.S. acts on its own without consulting others	35%	50%	85%
U.S. economic and trade pressures	21	47	68
Americans look down on Koreans	8	22	40
Envy of U.S. power and wealth	13	22	35
U.S. military intervention abroad	6	20	26
Presence of U.S. troops in Korea	5	10	15
Negative influences of U.S. culture and society	6	8	14
Hard-line U.S. policy toward North Korea	3	9	12
Issues form past (e.g., Kwangju, Nogun-Ri)	1	5	6
None of these	1	1	2
Don't know	2	2	4

Source: Office of Research, U.S. Department of State.

Table 4.5

Reasons People Dislike the United States, September 2003

"For what reason do people dislike America?"

Percent	Opinion
58%	Selfish pursuit of own interests and benefits
13.5	Disrespect toward Koreans and past problems
14.3	Dissatisfaction against U.S. forces stationed in Korea and military and diplomatic interference
4.5	Harsh policy against North Korea
1.3	Resistance against American society and culture
6.7	Show-off of its power and wealth
1.8	No answer

Source: *JoongAng Ilbo*-CSIS-RAND survey, September 2003, N=1,000.

Of policy interest is whether most Koreans view differences with the U.S. as being policy-related and therefore somewhat ephemeral (and remediable), or whether they reflect more basic incompatibilities in values (Figure 4.1).

As shown, when the Pew Research Center asked Koreans whether they thought differences between the U.S. were mostly due to different values or different policies, more than half mentioned policy differences, but a strong minority of

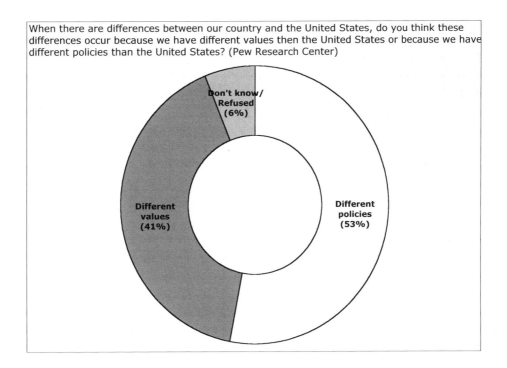

When there are differences between our country and the United States, do you think these differences occur because we have different values then the United States or because we have different policies than the United States? (Pew Research Center)

Don't know/ Refused (6%)

Different values (41%)

Different policies (53%)

Figure 4.1—Reason for Differences Between the U.S. and South Korea, August 2002

about four in ten said that they thought that they reflected differences in values, perhaps suggesting much deeper incompatibilities between the two countries.

Regarding specific policies, we also note a divergence in the views of South Koreans and Americans on the principal foci of U.S. national security for the foreseeable future: the North Korean threat and the U.S.'s war on terrorism. Although South Koreans seem to be only somewhat less alarmed than Americans about North Korea, they do not look at all favorably on the U.S. war on terrorism or the wars in Afghanistan or Iraq, whereas most Americans do (Table 4.6).[6]

In our research and various discussions of anti-American sentiment with experts, we also occasionally heard the argument that a key source of friction in U.S.-South Korean relations was South Koreans' personal dislike for President Bush. Pew actually asked a question about this, and the results do not lend particularly strong support to this explanation (Figure 4.2).

---

[6]More troubling still, 58 percent of those polled in South Korea actually expressed disappointment that the Iraqi military had put up so little resistance to the United States and its allies. Pew Research Center (2003), p. T-147. For an analysis of American public opinion toward the war on terrorism, see Larson and Savych (forthcoming).

As shown in the figure, only about one in five of those who had an unfavorable view of the U.S. in the summer of 2002 attributed it to President Bush, whereas nearly three out of four expressed the far more troubling view that it was the result of "a more general problem with America."[7]

Table 4.6
South Korean and American Attitudes on Key Security Issues

	South Koreans	Americans
View North Korea as a... [a]	69%	77%
Great danger	28	38
Moderate danger	41	39
View terrorism as a... [b]	44%	87%
Very big problem	15	50
Moderately big problem	29	37
Favor U.S. war on terrorism [a]	24%	89%
Agree with U.S. military action in Afghanistan [c]	43%	88%
Believe military action in Iraq justified [d]	20%	68%

SOURCES: [a] Pew Center for People and the Press, June 2003. [b] Pew Center for People and the Press, December 2002. [c] Gallup International, December 2001. [d] Gallup International, May 2003.

Taken together, many of these results are somewhat worrisome: Many South Koreans appear to share the generalized belief that their nation is not treated with respect by the U.S., substantial minorities have expressed the view that U.S.-South Korean differences are attributable to differences in values (which typically cannot be negotiated), and large majorities of those who had unfavorable opinions indicated that their unfavorable attitudes are not specific to the current administration.

---

[7]Because this question does not seem to have been asked before, it is impossible to say whether 20 percent is a little or a lot when compared to other past presidents. There are, however, some public opinion data suggesting that larger percentages had an unfavorable view of specific Bush administration actions. As we mentioned earlier, for example, about two out of three thought the January 2002 "axis of evil" speech was inappropriate. A plurality of 41 percent of those polled by the *Monthly Chosun* in December 2002 said that they preferred the Clinton administration policy on North Korea to the Bush administration policy, whereas only 32 percent preferred the Bush administration's policy. In June 2003, however, those polled by the *JoongAng Ilbo* were evenly divided on the Bush "hard policy " toward North Korea—48.5 percent favored the policy, while 48.4 percent opposed. *Monthly Chosun*, 12/1/02, N=1,000, and *JoongAng Ilbo*, 6/9-10/03, N=1,032. Even larger percentages believed that the Bush policy impeded an improvement of North-South relations. Unfortunately, we did not find any data that would have enabled any further comparisons of attitudes regarding Presidents Bush and Clinton.

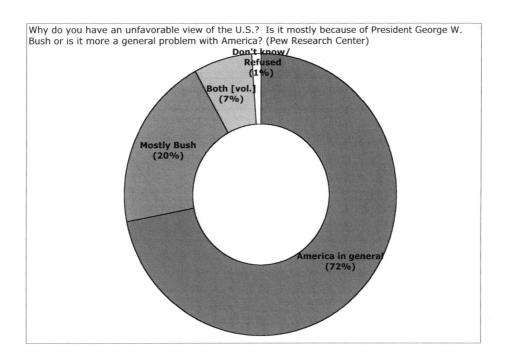

Figure 4.2—Reasons for Unfavorable View of the United States, August 2002

The Dynamics of Past Downturns in Favorable Sentiment

In Chapter 3, we identified three major downturns in favorable sentiment toward the U.S. We now describe in greater detail some of the apparent causes, manifestations, and resolution of these episodes.

The June 1995 Downturn in Favorable Sentiment

As described in the last chapter, the most likely proximate cause of the downturn in favorable sentiment toward the U.S. in June 1995 was the finalization of the implementing provisions of the October 1994 Agreed Framework in meetings between the U.S. and North Korea in Kuala Lumpur; this also came on the heels of a North Korean campaign to try to inflame political tensions in South Korea and U.S. market-opening pressures that also may have contributed.

As early as March 1995, polling by Gallup Korea found 56.8 percent who felt that in reaching the October 1994 agreement the U.S. had not taken into consideration the South Korean government's situation, and 58.7 percent said that the agreement would be meaningless if there were no inter-Korean talks on the matter.[8] Not surprisingly, the June 1995 U.S.-North Korean Kuala Lumpur agreement on implementation of the October 1994 Agreed Framework was viewed by many South Koreans as having ignored and excluded Seoul from another key agreement with the north on the nuclear issue, and led to reactions that generally ranged between irritation and anger at the U.S.

The matter seems to have been resolved when President Clinton gave Kim Young Sam assurances that South Korea would play a "key role" in the Light Water Reactor (LWR) issue, and as a result of the successful and well-received visit by Kim to Washington, D.C., in July 1995.

The February 2002 Downturn

Although there appear to have been other contributors—the U.S. war in Afghanistan, for example, and President Bush's January 29, 2003 State of the Union speech, in which North Korea was named as a member of the "axis of evil"—an incident during the 1,500 meter speed skating race in the 2002 Winter Olympics in Salt Lake City in February 2002 appears to have been largely responsible for the decline in favorable sentiment toward the U.S. at the time (the reader will recall that the data in Table 4.3 showed that about two-thirds of those polled cited the incident as a reason for less favorable sentiment).

The South Korean skater, Kim Dong-sung, was disqualified when a race judge (an Australian) ruled that he had interfered with the American, Apolo Ohno, when the U.S. skater had tried to pass on the final lap, prompting Ohno to throw up his hands. Despite an appeal by the South Korean Olympic Committee, the decision was upheld by the Court of Arbitration for Sport.[9]

Helped by the South Korean media,[10] the incident triggered a broad-based downturn in favorable sentiment toward the U.S. that reached well beyond the younger and better educated age groups that typically have held less favorable attitudes toward the U.S. (see Table 4.7). As shown, a majority of every age group under 50 years held an unfavorable opinion of the U.S., as did Koreans with who had graduated from high school or gone on to college; large percentages of those 50 and above or with a junior high school education or less

---

[8]Gallup Korea, March 29, 1995, excluding Jeju, Adults aged 20 and older, N=515.

[9]The Committee accepted the U.S. Olympic Committee's argument that South Korea "had no basis for alleging that the field of play decision was arbitrary or made in bad faith, Siddons (2002).

[10]For example, footage of the incident was in heavy rotation on Korean television, which frequently described Ohno's response to the South Korean skater as a "Hollywood action," i.e., an overly dramatic response to the South Korean skater's action.

either held unfavorable views, or were unable or unwilling to answer the question.

Table 4.7

Favorable and Unfavorable Sentiment Toward the United States, February 2002

Overall, do you have a very favorable, somewhat favorable, somewhat unfavorable, or very unfavorable opinion of the U.S.? (Gallup Korea, 2/26/02, Adults aged 20 and older, N=1,032)

	Very favorable	Somewhat favorable	Somewhat unfavorable	Very unfavorable	DK / Refused	Sample size
Total Sample	9.2%	24.4%	29.0%	30.6%	6.7%	1,032
			By Age Group			
20–29 yrs	4.8%	18.3%	28.8%	41.4%	6.7%	261
30–39 yrs	2.2	19.0	38.4	35.6	4.8	275
40–49 yrs	11.1	29.8	26.0	29.4	3.7	208
50+ yrs	18.6	31.4	22.5	16.9	10.6	288
			By Education			
Jr. high/under	19.8%	32.2%	19.5%	13.8%	14.7%	216
HS graduates	8.1	21.3	32.0	32.8	5.9	369
College/upper	5.1	23.3	31.2	37.0	3.5	447
College Students	0.0%	0.0%	40.7%	59.3%	0.0%	7

Source: Gallup Korea Ltd., http://panel.gallup.co.kr.

The incident also led to boycotts of U.S. businesses in South Korea, increased opposition to the then-pending sale of U.S. F-15 fighter aircraft,[11] growth in the number of anti-American internet sites in South Korea,[12] and a number of other expressions of anti-American sentiment, including the release of a song (called "F***ing U.S.A.") that was highly derogatory of the U.S. and soon became an underground hit in South Korea.[13]

That the outcome of a sports match could result in such an outpouring of animus toward the U.S. is only somewhat less surprising than the fact that many young South Koreans apparently embraced the song and its anti-American sentiments.

---

[11]The ROK Ministry of National Defense website was flooded with bulletin board postings opposing the purchase of U.S. F-15s. See Yonhap, February 22, 2002.

[12]According to one report, more than 100 anti-American Internet sites were created in the wake of the incident. See Ho-t'aek (2002), and KCNA, April 4, 2002.

[13]See Pyong-kyu (2002). A music video from a Korean pop girl-group called S.E.S. that revolved around band members' fantasies about punishing arrogant Americans also was released at about this time. See Deguervian (2002).

76

The December 2002 Downturn

Although there seems to have been a slight recovery in favorable sentiment by August 2002,[14] a second downturn in favorable sentiment occurred sometime around December 2002. Although our trend data suggest this decline in favorable sentiment failed to reach the nadir set in the February 2002 downturn, we judge this incident to be the more serious one of the two.[15]

This episode followed the acquittal, in late November, of two U.S. servicemen who drove an armored vehicle that accidentally killed two South Korean schoolgirls in June 2002,[16] and came at the height of a presidential campaign in which then-MDP candidate Roh successfully cultivated the support of young and progressive South Koreans and others who generally were predisposed toward less favorable attitudes toward the U.S. (see Table 4.7), and whose anti-American sentiment already was on the rise as a result of the acquittal.[17]

Candlelight vigils—a form of honoring the deaths of the schoolgirls, expressing sentiment in favor of a revision to the Status of Forces Agreement (SOFA), and expressing broader anti-U.S. sentiment—were widespread by this time, and other anti-U.S. activity also was on the rise.[18] Thus, while the public opinion data presented earlier suggested that the February 2002 downturn was slightly more severe than that in December 2002, the mobilization of large numbers of South Koreans during the latter period suggests that the public opinion data underestimate the severity of this downturn; many observers believe, with good reason, that the December 2002 downturn was far more consequential.

Importantly, suggestions by then-President Kim Dae Jung,[19] president-elect Roh Mu-hyon,[20] former president Kim Young-sam,[21] and the mainstream South

---

[14]Polling by the Pew Research Center and Gallup Korea in August 2002 showed the percentage of South Koreans holding favorable views of the U.S. rose to 53 percent, a nearly 20-point increase over the February 2002 reading. The recovery suggests that the issue of the schoolgirls' deaths had not yet become a salient factor in South Koreans' judgments about the U.S.

[15]As was mentioned earlier, the timing of the February 2002 poll was at a time when emotions were running high in South Korea; it is not clear exactly when emotions peaked in the December 2002 downturn.

[16]It seems to have taken some time for the incident to become highly salient to South Koreans, and it was not until the acquittal was announced that South Koreans took to the streets.

[17] See Sang-chu (2002a, 2002b, 2002c).

[18]For example, postings at dissident and anti-U.S. web sites seem to have increased.

[19]See "ROK President Calls on Cabinet to 'Discuss Ways' to Revise SOFA, Stresses USFK's Role," Yonhap, December 3, 2002, Chae-yong (2002), and "ROK President Says Recent Poll Showed Public's Opposition to USFK Withdrawal," Chosun Ilbo, January 8, 2003.

[20]See "ROK President-elect Calls for End to Anti-U.S. Candlelight Vigils," Yonhap, December 28, 2002.

[21]"The Elders Speak Out," Joongang Ilbo, January 18, 2003.

Korean press[22] that the candlelight vigils and other demonstrations were harmful to South Korea's interests seem to have been ignored.[23] The demonstrations did not actually stop until reports emerged that unless the situation improved the U.S. itself might consider withdrawing its forces from Korea.[24]

A Model of South Korean Attitudes Toward the U.S.

The historical analysis in Chapter 2, the analysis of trends in Chapter 3, and the foregoing brief review of South Koreans' own explanations of the sources of friction in the U.S-South Korean relationship suggest that there are many potential sources for favorable and unfavorable sentiment toward the U.S.

We now describe the results of our statistical modeling, which provides a simple but powerful and policy-relevant way of explaining favorable and unfavorable sentiment toward the U.S. among South Koreans. Following the discussion of the model and its parameters, we will identify a number of other factors that could help to explain the remaining variation in sentiment toward the U.S., but due to data limitations were impossible to include in our statistical modeling.

Approach

To develop a coherent explanation for favorable and unfavorable sentiment toward the U.S., we first conducted a number of correlation and regression analyses using the trend data from the U.S. State Department for the 1988–2001 period (reported in Figures 3.3 and 3.4) to see which combination of potential predictors did the best job in accounting for variance in the trend for favorable and unfavorable sentiment toward the U.S. at the ecological (aggregate) level.

---

[22]See Tae-chung (October 21, 2002 and October 22, 2002); "Even the President-Elect Is Appealing for Restraining of Demonstrations," *Dong-A Ilbo*, December 30, 2002; "Importance of Korea-U.S. Alliance; Closer Cooperation Needed to Cope With Nuclear Crisis," *The Korea Times*, December 30, 2002; "ROK Media Leaders Worry 'Intense' Anti-Americanism, Call for 'Closer' ROK-US Ties," *The Korea Times*, January 9, 2003; Hyong-ki (2003); and "We Have Been Heard," *JoongAng Ilbo*, December 30, 2002. Somewhat predictably, the left-leaning and U.S.-critical *Hankyore* endorsed continuation of the demonstrations. See "Candlelight Demonstrations Are Energy for Peace," *Hankyoreh*, December 30, 2002.

[23]For example, 88 percent of those who participated in an online poll at the Pomdaewi website in early January 2003 said that in spite of calls for a halt to the candlelight vigils, they should continue. See Chong-mu (2003).

[24]In mid-February 2003, Secretary of Defense Rumsfeld suggested that some U.S. forces in South Korea might be withdrawn, and others moved. This was widely interpreted as a signal of U.S. displeasure toward the growing anti-American sentiment in South Korea. See Efron and Magnier (2003), Cable News Network (2003), and Chong-won (2002).

These analyses suggested that about 80 percent of the variance in the aggregate trend data could be explained using only two variables: (1) South Koreans' opinions on U.S.-South Korean relations at the time (the wording and data are reported in Figures 3.6 and 3.7), and (2) the importance of U.S. forces to protecting Korean security (wording and data reported in Figures 3.9 and 3.10).[25] An interpretation consistent with these findings is that fleeting reactions to specific bilateral developments are constrained (or dampened) by longer-term concerns about the importance of U.S. forces to South Korea's security. Moreover, most of the variance in the percentage who thought U.S. forces were unimportant to South Korea's security could be accounted for by the percentage who found the threat of attack from the north unlikely.[26]

Using several datasets from polling done by the U.S. State Department in the early 1990s, and the multivariate statistical technique of logistic regression (suitable for dichotomous dependent variables), we then tested this model with respondent-level data to see whether the aggregate-level relationship also held at the individual-level.[27] Finally, we tested the robustness of the model over time by estimating comparable models with more recent survey data from the State Department. This work shows that the model had even higher explanatory power with more recent data than with the data from the early 1990s period.

Description of the Model

As described earlier, although individual South Koreans differ in their diagnoses of the causes of friction in U.S.-South Korean relations and appear to weigh ephemeral influences against longer-term interests in a somewhat ad hoc fashion, favorable and unfavorable sentiment can be accurately predicted by a relatively simple model that balances short- and long-term concerns (see Figure 4.3).

As shown in the figure, the basic model is quite parsimonious, and predicts individuals' opinion toward the U.S. based upon two main variables: (1) opinion on the current state of U.S.-South Korean relations (which we conjecture is in turn predicted by the balance of positive and negative developments in U.S.-

---

[25]Our regression modeling showed that 80 percent of the variance in the ecological (aggregate-level) data could be accounted for by these two variables, the t-statistics on the coefficients for both variables, and the F-statistic for the overall model were all statistically significant.

[26]In a simple regression of the aggregate (ecological) data, 60 percent of the variance in the importance of U.S. forces to Korean security was accounted for by beliefs about the threat from the north. Put another way, one can account for 60 percent of the variation in the percentage who believe U.S. forces are unimportant simply by knowing the percentage who don't find North Korea very threatening.

[27]To impute such a relationship at the individual level from aggregate-level data would be committing what is commonly called the "ecological fallacy."

South Korean relations at any time),[28] and (2) judgments about the importance of U.S. forces in protecting South Korea (which is in turn predicted by assessments of the threat from the north, the regional military balance, and the credibility of the U.S. security commitment, and the prospects for peaceful reunification).[29]

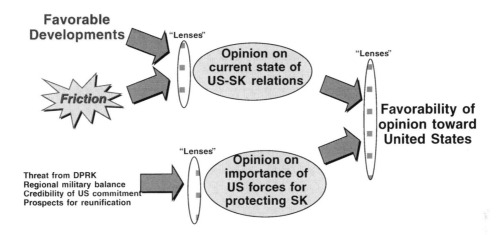

Figure 4.3—Model of South Korean Attitudes Toward the United States

As might be expected, the first parameter is subject to some volatility as a result of its sensitivity to both positive and negative developments; the second parameter, on the other hand, buoys favorable sentiment, and introduces a measure of stability in favorable attitudes that otherwise would be lacking.

These influences are filtered through South Koreans' "lenses"—age, education, nationalism, ideology, and other factors—that operate at the individual level to magnify, diminish, or otherwise color the significance of specific developments, perceived changes in threat, and other factors, or otherwise predispose individuals to hold favorable or unfavorable views of the U.S.

---

[28]Some of the best work on what moves American public opinion on policy issues suggest that the U.S. media normally take cues from government officials, "indexing" coverage to the range of opinions that exist within the government, and that mass opinion tends to follow elite opinion, with the most politically attentive members of the public following elites most closely. The extent to which this might be true in South Korean society is unknown, which means that the "favorable developments" and "frictions" in the figure are a conjecture, albeit one with empirical support in another society; this obviously is a very fruitful area for future research. For excellent works in this area, see Zaller (1992) and Brody (1992).

[29]Our model predicted overall favorable and unfavorable sentiment based upon a total of five independent variables that were considered simultaneously: (1) opinion on the state of U.S.-Korean relations, the question wording for which was reported in Figures 3.6 and 3.7; (2) the importance of U.S. forces to South Korea's security, the question wording for which was reported in Figures 3.9 and 3.10; age; education; and political party. The first two variables were the most important predictors. Detailed descriptions of these variables are provided in Savych and Larson (2004).

Our logistic regression models correctly predicted favorable or unfavorable attitudes for anywhere from 65 to 73 percent of the respondents in the April 1990, October 1991, September 1993, June 1995, and July 2001 surveys;[30] the models also correctly classified 67 percent of the respondents in a June 1995 survey, and 73 percent of the respondents in a July 2001 survey. Also as predicted, 66-73 percent of respondents' positions on the importance of U.S. forces to Korea's security could be correctly classified on the basis of their beliefs about the threat of a North Korean attack, the regional military balance, and confidence that the U.S. would help South Korea if attacked.

We determined that these models suggested that South Koreans' most basic attitudes toward the U.S. were sensibly related,[31] and subject to a number of policy-relevant constraints. and that they demonstrated sufficient accuracy and robustness over time in predicting favorable or unfavorable attitudes toward the U.S. that they were suitable as a tool for reasoning about the likely path of South Koreans' attitudes toward the U.S. in response to different sorts of developments.

Influences on Opinions of U.S.-Korean Relations

As described in Chapter 2, South Koreans' opinions on the U.S.-South Korean relationship derive from a great many sources.

Some of these influences are to be found in the daily stream of new developments that affect South Koreans' calculations about what the U.S.-South Korean relationship can (or should) be (the favorable developments and frictions noted in Figure 4.3), and the extent to which new developments suggest healthy growth or emerging problems: developments related to North-South relations, actions taken or not taken by South Korea, the U.S., and North Korea, and nationalistic or sensationalistic media reporting all can affect Koreans' assessments of the bilateral relationship.

Other factors—described in Figure 4.3 as "lenses"—are to be found within individuals themselves, many of which can affect the probability of being aware of new events, and can greatly color how new events are interpreted. These include the specific historical residue that individuals use to filter new developments, perceived security and economic vulnerabilities, nationalism, and

---

[30]Typically, logistic regression models did slightly better than ordered logistic regression models. The detailed results of our modeling can be found in Savych and Larson (2004).

[31]For an excellent discussion of rationality in American public opinion, see Page and Shapiro (1992). For complementary analyses of the processes by which American mass attitudes diffuse, see Neuman (1986), Brody (1992), and Zaller (1992).

a variety of factors associated with generational, educational, and social differences. Some of these will be described in greater detail later in this chapter.

And importantly, reactions can vary greatly depending upon how directly new developments appear to directly threaten South Korean's sense of sovereignty and national pride—which can lead to a reflexive, nationalistic response—or instead provide evidence of due consideration in the bilateral relationship.

Influences on Assessments of the Importance of U.S. Forces

The influences on assessments of the importance of U.S. forces are somewhat more straightforward. As we described in Figure 4.3 and in our discussion of the modeling, the importance of U.S. forces to Korean security is generally tied to beliefs about threats and needed responses, which include consideration of the nature of the threat from the north and the prospects for peaceful reunification, the nature of the North-South military balance, and the credibility of U.S. security guarantees.[32] More generally, we would expect—and indeed, as the data in Tables 3.2 through 3.4 suggested—that consideration of other long-term regional threats (e.g., from China, Japan, or Russia) and responses also could play an important role in judgments about the future importance of U.S. forces.

The Threat From North Korea

As just described, our statistical work suggests that beliefs about the threat from the north is an important predictor of the importance of U.S. forces in protecting South Korean security.

Figures 4.4 and 4.5 report the available trend data on South Koreans' views of the threat from the north; the time series end in 1999, when the State Department stopped asking this question.

As shown in Figure 4.4, South Koreans historically have been fairly optimistic about the threat from the north; only on one occasion between 1988 and 1999 (February 1997) did concern about the threat eclipse optimism, and that was quite short-lived.

When these data are broken out by strength of feeling (Figure 4.5), it is clear that chronic worriers about the threat from the north are in the distinct minority—only about 5 percent—whereas those who are least concerned

---

[32]About 60 percent of the variance in the trend data for the importance of U.S. forces to protecting South Korean security could be accounted for by the trend data on the perceived threat from the north. Our respondent-level multivariate statistical modeling was able to correctly predict beliefs about the importance of U.S. forces for anywhere from 56 to 79 percent of the respondents.

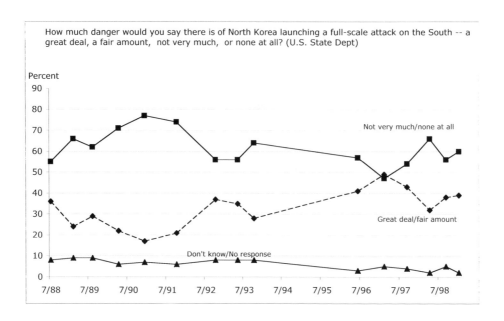

Figure 4.4—Danger of a North Korean Attack in the Next Three Years, 1988–1999

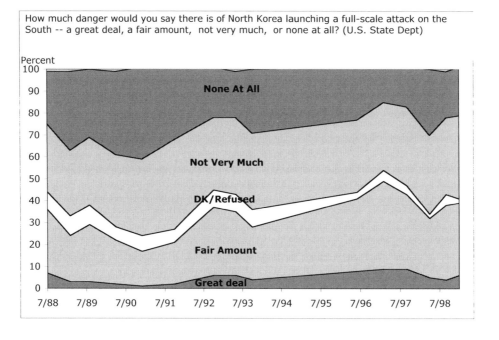

Figure 4.5—Danger of a North Korean Attack in the Next Three Years, 1988–1999

(the dark panel at the top) constitute anywhere from 20 to 40 percent of the public. Most South Koreans—anywhere from 55 to 75 percent—fall in the middle, neither particularly alarmed nor particularly optimistic.

Although the trend data are available only to 1999, other polling suggests that following the June 2000 summit between the two Kims, concerns about the prospects of war remained low or even declined: polling by *The Hankyoreh 21* in June 2000 and March 2002 found 89 and 81 percent who said that it was very or somewhat impossible that war could break out on the Korean peninsula.[33] Fifty-nine percent of those polled by *Dong-A Ilbo* in October 2000 thought war on the peninsula was impossible,[34] polling by Gallup Korea in November 2002 and February 2003 found 58 and 56 percent who thought a war very or somewhat unlikely,[35] and the September 2003 *JoongAng Ilbo*-CSIS-RAND survey found 64 percent who thought the prospect of war with the north in the next three years was not really possible or not at all possible.[36]

Figure 4.6 presents some additional data from the U.S. State Department that asked South Koreans about the threat from the North in the event that economic sanctions were imposed on North Korea.

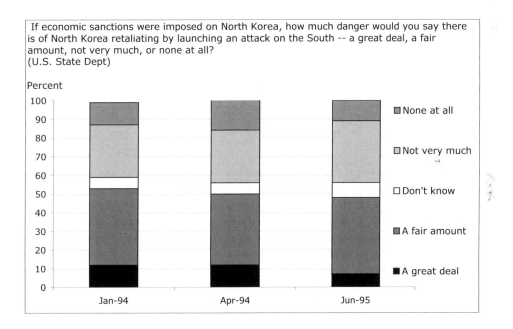

Figure 4.6—Danger of Attack If Economic Sanctions Are Imposed, 1994–1995

[33]*The Hankyoreh 21*, July 18, 2000, reporting on polling done on June 26, 2000, N=700, and *The Hankyoreh 21*, March 12, 2002, reporting on polling done on March 8-9, 2002, N=500.

[34]*Dong-A Ilbo*, December 5, 2000, reporting polling on October 25-November 2000, N=2,000.

[35]Gallup Korea, November 2, 2002, N=1,040, and February 24, 2003, N=1,013.

[36]*JoongAng Ilbo*-CSIS-RAND survey, September 15–17, 2003, N=1,000.

As shown, when compared to the data for the period in Figure 4.5, these data suggest that the prospect of economic sanctions on the north elicited the belief that the danger from the north might increase as a result: whereas 30–35 percent expressed concern during this period in Figure 4.5, about half did so when the possibility of sanctions was suggested. Given that economic sanctions remain a distinct possibility if there is a breakdown in the six-party talks with North Korea, we expect that many South Koreans would respond in an equally cautious manner to the suggestion today.

Using the Chi-square test of independence, we also assessed the direct relationship between the belief that North Korea was a threat to the stability of Asia and world peace and a favorable attitude toward the U.S. (Table 4.8).

As shown—and as predicted by our statistical modeling—those who were more inclined to view North Korea as a threat also were more likely to hold favorable views of the U.S., and this relationship was statistically significant: the p-value for the Chi-square test was highly significant.

Table 4.8

Cross-Tabulation of Favorable Attitude Toward U.S. and Belief That North Korea Is a Threat to Stability

Opinion on U.S.	-----North Korean Danger to Stability of Asia and World Peace-----				
	Great Danger	Moderate Danger	Small Danger	No Danger At All	DK/Ref
Very favorable	6%	2%	3%	0%	6%
Somewhat favorable	54	43	37	24	28
Somewhat unfavorable	28	41	46	46	44
Very unfavorable	9	10	12	21	6
DK/Refused	3	4	2	9	17
				p-value for Chi-square test:	<.005

Source: Pew Research Center Global Attitudes Survey, May 2003, N=525.
NOTE: Question wordings were as follows: "Please tell me if you have a very favorable, somewhat favorable, somewhat unfavorable or very unfavorable opinion of the United States" and "How much of a danger is the current government in North Korea is to the stability of Asia and world peace? A great danger, moderate danger, small danger, or no danger at all?"

Finally, it is worth mentioning that although some polling has suggested that a high percentage of South Koreans believe that the north has nuclear weapons,[37] only a minority appear to believe that these weapons are aimed at South Korea. In polling by Gallup Korea in December 2002, 28 percent said they thought that if North Korea developed nuclear weapons, those weapons would be aimed at the South, whereas 54 percent said they would aimed at an unspecified "other country," presumably the U.S.[38] Students, younger and better-educated South Koreans were less likely to believe that North Korea would target the South.

The Military Balance: Relative South-North Capabilities and U.S. Credibility

Our modeling suggested that beliefs about the military balance between the two Koreas, i.e., the South's ability to prevail in a one-on-one contest against the North, and the credibility of the U.S. security commitment to South Korea, are key predictors of the importance of U.S. forces to protecting South Korea.[39]

Although there were no trend data available on this matter, a recent poll by the Hyundai Research Institute suggests that about six in ten South Koreans (60.2 percent) believe that when U.S. forces' contribution to the defense of South Korea is netted out, the north-south military balance favors the North.[40] The Hyundai Research Institute poll also asked a question about the credibility of the U.S. commitment (Table 4.9). As shown, 87 percent of South Koreans believe that the U.S. would honor its security commitments in the event of a crisis with North Korea, whereas 12 percent think the U.S. would remain neutral, and fewer than 1 percent think the U.S. would support the North. Although eight in ten or more in each group expressed a belief in the credibility of the U.S. security commitment, the data also show some differences in responses by age.

These findings help to clarify the reason that U.S. forces are viewed as important to so many South Koreans and suggest that, were South Koreans to decide that

---

[37]For example, a September 1997 poll by JoongAng Ilbo found 39.4 percent who said it was very possible and 43 percent who said it was somewhat possible that North Korea had nuclear weapons. *JoongAng Ilbo*, September 24, 1997, N=1,200.

[38]Gallup Korea, December 24, 2002, Adults aged 20 and over, N=1,063.

[39]As was described earlier, our aggregate-level regression modeling showed that about 60 percent of the variance in the aggregate trend data on the importance of U.S. forces to Korean security could be accounted for by the aggregate trend data on the perceived threat from the north. Our individual-level modeling correctly predicted beliefs about the importance of U.S. forces for 61 to 73 percent of the respondents largely based upon respondents' estimates of South Korea's military strength, the danger they perceived of an attack form the north, and confidence that the U.S. would help in an attack. Age, education, and party also were included in the model. For details of the datasets and the modeling see Savych and Larson (forthcoming).

[40]Hyundai Research Institute asked: "Without U.S. forces what do you think of the military balance between North Korea and South Korea?" A total of 60.2 percent thought the north was superior, 17.8 percent thought they had similar capabilities, and 19.7 percent said that the South was superior. See Hyundai Research Institute (2003).

the military balance actually favored the South (e.g., as a result of a program to develop an independent national defense capability) or that the U.S. was unlikely to honor its security commitments, their belief in the importance of the U.S. military contribution could be eroded, and the percentage of South Koreans who hold favorable attitudes toward the U.S. could be reduced. This is somewhat ironic, given the U.S.'s strong support for a policy of improving South Korean military capabilities. *[Better to say exactly what policy here.]*

Table 4.9

South Koreans' Evaluation of the Credibility of the U.S. Security Commitment

"Will the U.S. support South Korea in the event of a crisis with North Korea?"

	Support ROK	Neutral	Support DPRK
Total sample	87.1%	12.0%	0.8%
Age			
18–29 yrs	83.9	14.6	1.6
30–39 yrs	85.3	14.1	0.6
40–49 yrs	90.1	9.5	0.4
50+ yrs	92.7	6.8	0.6

Source: Hyundai Research Institute (2003), which reports on polling done June 13–July 4, 2003, face-to-face interviews with adults age 18–59 years, N=1,187.

Prospects for Reunification

Although we were not able to include any data regarding South Koreans' expectations for reunification in our respondent-level statistical modeling, we conjecture that views about the importance of U.S. forces to protecting South Korea's security also would be tied to optimism or pessimism about the prospects for peaceful reunification: the stronger the belief that the peninsula would be reunified peacefully, we hypothesize, the lower the perceived importance of U.S. forces.

The best trend data that are available suggest that there has been a fairly steep decline in optimism regarding the prospects for reunification (see Figure 4.7).[41]

As shown in the figure, which presents data from polling by *JoongAng Ilbo* from 1994 to 2002, the percentage of South Koreans who expected reunification in 10 years or fewer plummeted from about 60 percent in 1994 to about 30 percent in

---

[41]Polling by the Korean Institute for National Unification in 1993, 1994, and 1999 shows a similar trend.

2002. Meanwhile, the percentage expecting reunification in 10 to 20 years or more than 20 years generally rose, with a little more than 30 percent expecting reunification in 10–20 years, and a bit less than 20 percent expecting reunification in 20 years or more. After bottoming out at about 5 percent during the exuberant period of the Sunshine Policy during 1998–2000, the percentage of those deeming reunification impossible has more recently climbed to nearly 20 percent.

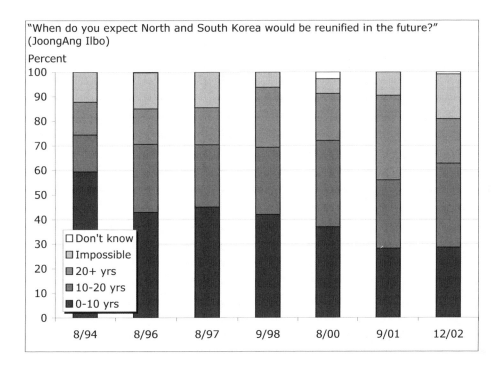

Figure 4.7—Expectations Regarding Reunification

The most recent snapshot of attitudes toward reunification comes from the September 2003 *JoongAng Ilbo*-CSIS-RAND survey (Table 4.10), which suggests that about six in ten South Koreans still think reunification is possible, and a majority of these think that the alliance with the U.S. should be maintained after reunification. It is likely that a large percentage of those who believe that reunification is not possible also favor continuation of the alliance with the U.S., but the question did not ask these respondents about the alliance.

The Longer-Term Security Outlook

Finally, to be complete, we simply note that if or when the threat from the north recedes,[42] South Koreans will face what may be a much more complex security environment. In such an environment, the continued presence of U.S. military forces in South Korea may help to underwrite stability and security in a region that still involves historical animosities and regional rivalries.[43]

Table 4.10

Views on the Possibility of Reunification, September 2003

"Do you see reunification as possible? If possible, do you think maintaining the military alliance with the U.S. is necessary after reunification?

62%	Reunification possible, if so
33	Maintain the alliance
29	No need to maintain the alliance
37	Reunification not possible
2	Not sure

Source: *JoongAng Ilbo*-CSIS-RAND poll, September 15–17, 2003, N=1,000.

Aside from the mention of the potential Chinese and Japanese threats by a tiny percentage of respondents as a reason that it is necessary that U.S. forces remain in South Korea, reported in Tables 3.2 through 3.4, there is scant evidence that most South Koreans have given serious consideration to the long-term possibility that it may be desirable for U.S. forces to continue to play a balancing and stabilizing role.[44]

Predictions of the Model

Our model has important implications for policy and diplomacy toward South Korea, including public diplomacy, and can be used to make contingent

---

[42]To paraphrase Mark Twain's famous observation, rumors of North Korea's imminent death have been greatly exaggerated over the past decade, and North Korea has proved itself remarkably resilient in the face of predictions of its imminent demise.

[43]Indeed, China recently made public statements that suggested to South and North Koreans alike that it was laying the groundwork for making a historically-based claim for the Korean peninsula. See Faiola (2004). For a discussion of future challenges facing the alliance, see Treverton, Larson, and Kim (2003).

[44]It is worth mentioning that if it were to become a recurring theme or the official ROK government position, the statement by President Roh that "When we say U.S. troops will leave, it does not mean that they will go soon. However, they will not stay for 10 or 20 years, either" could erode the belief that U.S. forces remain important to South Korea's security. See T'ae-hyon (2003).

predictions—some obvious, and some less so—about the likely path of South Korean attitudes toward the U.S. in response to specific developments.

To apply the model, one must translate a potential development into its likely effect on the parameters of the model, and assess the likely effect on favorable sentiment toward the U.S. To illustrate how the model might be used to make policy-relevant predictions, it makes the following contingent predictions (under the usual assumptions that all else is equal):[45]

- Favorable sentiment toward the U.S. is likely to increase as a result of U.S.-South Korean summits, agreements on common positions, and other developments that are presented as successes for Korea, as reflecting "equality," "balance," and "fairness" in the relationship, or as preserving or enhancing Korean sovereignty.

- Favorable sentiment is likely to decline in response to developments that accent irreconcilable U.S.-South Korean differences, expressions of U.S. superiority, high-handedness, or arrogance, or developments that are perceived as encroachments of Korean sovereignty, or suggest that South Korea has somehow "lost" in an encounter with the U.S.

- Favorable sentiment is likely to increase as a result of North Korean threats and provocations seemingly unrelated to U.S. actions, but may decline where these threats and provocations in fact appear to be a response to (or lead to) undesirable stridency on the part of the U.S., i.e., where the U.S. itself is perceived to be engaging in undesired escalatory behavior.

- Increased turbulence in favorable sentiment—or even a decline—would be expected in response to developments that suggest that the threat from the North is declining. In the short term, this might be a result of North Korean "charm offensives," highly symbolic concessions on reunification issues, or other similar developments; in the long term, reunification of the two Koreas would be expected to eliminate the perceived threat from the north, reduce the perceived importance of the U.S., and reduce favorable sentiment toward the U.S.

- President Roh's recently announced desire for an "independent national defense" capability actually could lead either to greater turbulence or a reduction in favorable sentiment toward the U.S., for two reasons. First, increased turbulence or declines in favorable sentiment might result from the

---

[45]This includes the assumption that there are no major changes in the basic structure of South Korean attitudes toward the U.S., and that the relationships between the variables, and their constraining influence on one another, continue to hold just as they have for the last dozen or more years. Of course, if there were a fundamental change in attitude structures, the model's predictive ability could be greatly weakened. In such a case, a new model would need to be estimated.

improvement in the local military balance with the north, and the reduction in the perceived importance of U.S. forces to Korean security that would be expected to result from that. Second, favorable sentiment could decline to the extent that South Koreans view the financial burdens associated with improved defense as somehow "unfair."

- Either declines in favorable sentiment or increased turbulence would be expected to the extent that beliefs about the credibility of the U.S.'s security commitment to Korea had eroded among South Koreans, as that credibility is an important predictor of the belief that U.S. forces are important to Korea's security.

- In cases of developments that move in opposite directions (e.g., where the perceived threat from the north increases but the credibility of the U.S. security commitment also declines) the result is likely to be indeterminate.

These predictions of the model are illustrative, not exhaustive, but suggest a wide range of applications for diagnosis and contingent prediction.

Individual-Level Lenses

Our logistic regression models did a fairly good job predicting favorable or unfavorable opinion among South Koreans using a small number of variables: we were able to correctly predict favorable or unfavorable opinions for two-thirds to three-quarters of the respondents in the U.S. State Department's polling over the last dozen years relying on two key variables—assessments of the state of U.S.-South Korean relations and the importance of U.S. forces to protecting South Korean security—but also including three lenses: age and education, and party. There are, in fact, a number of factors that we found to be associated with favorable and unfavorable sentiment on a bivariate basis that might help to further explain differences in sentiment. We begin by describing these factors, and then, later in this chapter, identify potential influences on them that are to be found in the larger South Korean society.

As was described in Figure 4.3, we came to think of a number of individual-level characteristics—age, education, student status, ideological or party orientation, media use, and so on—as potential lenses that might magnify or diminish the importance of events and developments as they occur:

- In some cases, as with younger, better-educated, and left-leaning South Koreans, these lenses may lead them to magnify the importance of negative developments in U.S.-South Korean relations, and either overlook or discount the importance of positive ones.

- In other cases, as with older, less well-educated, and more religious or conservative South Koreans, these lenses might lead them to do just the opposite, i.e., magnify the importance of positive developments, and diminish or discount the importance of negative ones.

Given that individuals differ in their interest in politics and can choose from among many different newspapers, broadcast radio and television stations, Internet web sites, and other information channels, and that individuals with different background might pick out different developments as significant and weigh their importance differently, it is easy to see how the same event might impact different South Koreans in different ways. Even if we are unable to include all of them in our modeling, it is important to understand which of these lenses have the prospect of being systematically associated with differences in favorable and unfavorable sentiment toward the U.S.

We next discuss four of these lenses: age, education, student status, and media consumption habits. We also report the results of our analysis of another characteristic—regionalism—that appeared to be only modestly associated with favorable and unfavorable sentiment toward the U.S.

Age

One of the most widely cited findings in past analyses of public opinion toward the U.S. is that age is an important individual-level predictor of sentiment: younger South Koreans consistently have had less favorable views of the U.S. than older South Koreans. Our analyses confirm this as a very robust finding.

Figure 4.8 presents the percentages saying they had an unfavorable opinion of the U.S. in 17 polls conducted by the State Department between 1988 and 2001. As shown, the general trend is downward—as the age of the respondents increases, the percentages with unfavorable views declines.[46] Polling by Gallup Korea in 1993, 1994, and 2002 showed a similar result: in all cases, the pattern was the same—favorable and unfavorable sentiment were closely associated with age, and the result was statistically significant.[47]

---

[46]Note that the June 1995 poll revealed a broad-based increase in unfavorable sentiment.

[47]We performed a Chi-square test of independence on the question asked by Gallup Korea in September 1993, September 1994, and February 2002 that asked respondents "Overall, do you have a very favorable, somewhat favorable, somewhat unfavorable, or very unfavorable opinion of the U.S.?" In all three cases, the Chi-square test yielded a statistically significant result (at the .001 level), suggesting that favorable and unfavorable sentiment were associated with age, and that the relationship was a robust one. The data can be found in Savych and Larson (2004).

The importance of age as a discriminator in attitudes toward the U.S. can also be seen in other U.S.-relevant attitudes. For example, age also is associated with opinions on the state of U.S.-South Korean relations and the importance of U.S. forces to protecting South Korean security and with beliefs about whether the U.S. or North Korea constitutes the greater threat to Korea (Figures 4.9 and 4.10).

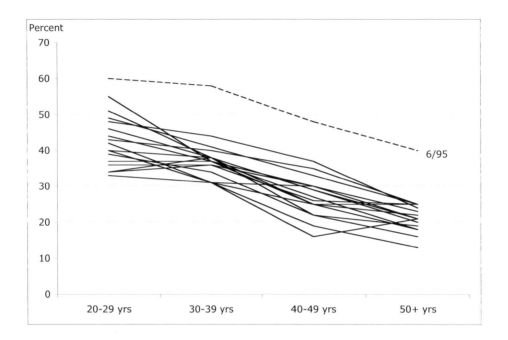

Figure 4.8—Percentage Unfavorable by Age in State Department Polling, 1998–2001

As shown in Figures 4.9 and 4.10, the percentage identifying North Korea as the greater threat to South Korea increases with age, and the percentage identifying the U.S. as the greater threat declines.[48] Indeed, fully 50 percent of those 30 or younger in the Korea Barometer survey identified the U.S. as the greater threat, while only about 20 percent of the 60-somethings did so; the results were nearly as striking for the Gallup Korea data.

---

[48]A Chi-square test of the data in Figure 4.9 demonstrated a statistically significant relationship between favorable sentiment and age, at the .001 level. We were unable to perform a Chi-square test on the data in Figure 4.10, as we lacked the necessary information on subgroup sizes.

Birth Cohort Analysis

When discussing anti-American sentiment, many are quick to identify "the 386 generation"—in their 30s in the 1990s, pro-democracy university students in the 1980s, and born in the 1960s.[49] Although the data presented in Figures 4.8 through 4.10 suggest that 20-somethings usually have had the least favorable attitudes toward the U.S., claims are often heard that the 386 group is the age group with the least favorable views toward the U.S. While such results occasionally were observed (see Figure 4.8), most often it was the 20-somethings who held the least favorable attitudes.

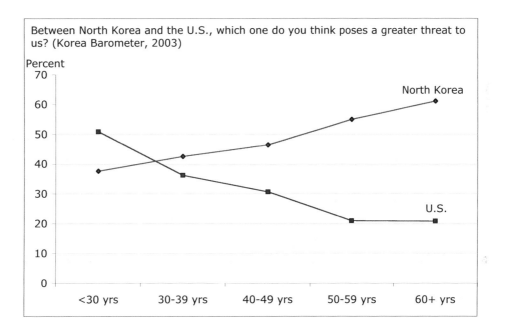

Figure 4.9—Views of Threat to South Korea by Age

---

[49]When the 386 generation were undergraduate students, South Korea was under a military regime and there was a substantial student movement that opposed the regime. There also were study groups, secretly organized by students, whose anti-Americanism was structural in nature, deriving from their progressive (or leftist) analyses. The anti-Americanism of the current generation of university students (the "Red Devils") generally is described as somewhat more sentimental than analytic and structural in nature, and, judging from the reaction to the February 2002 skating incident, presumably more sensitive to ephemeral events.

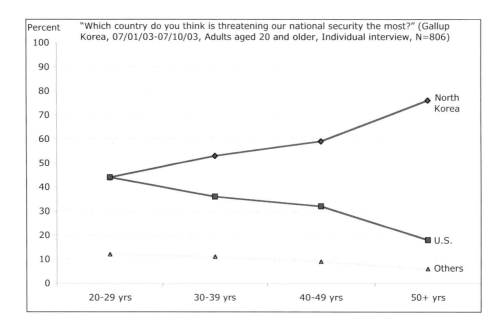

Figure 4.10—Country Posing the Greatest Threat to Korea, by Age

We were very interested in understanding the extent to which South Koreans in general—but especially the 386ers—continued to carry their unfavorable views of their youth into middle age. To better understand cohort effects over time, we compared unfavorable sentiment toward the U.S. from a number of State Department surveys approximately 10 years apart (see Tables 4.11 and 4.12).

Table 4.11

Age Group Analysis of Unfavorable Opinion of U.S. 1991–2002

UNFAVORABLE OPINION OF U.S. BY AGE GROUP (%UNFAVORABLE)

Age	October 1991	October 1992	July 2001	February 2002
20–29	54.7%	44.2%	36.4%	70.2%
30–39	37.0	37.3	35.9	70.4
40–49	24.8	26.9	26.3	55.4
50+	24.8	18.1	24.5	39.4
All	37.4%	34.2%	31.6%	59.6%

SOURCE: Office of Research, U.S. Department of State (10/91, 10/92, and 7/01 data), and Gallup Korea (2/02 data).

As shown in Table 4.11, unfavorable sentiment was lowest in July 2001 and highest in February 2002, with the by-now familiar age effects described earlier. Table 4.12 computes the change over time for each birth cohort, i.e., it compares the views of those who were 30–39 years of age in 1991–1992 with their views when they were 40–49 years in 2001–2002.[50]

Table 4.12

Cohort Analysis of Change in Unfavorable Opinion 1991–2002

CHANGE IN UNFAVORABLE OPINION OF U.S. BY AGE GROUP (% UNFAVORABLE)

Age in 1991–1992	October 1991– July 2001	October 1991– February 2002	October 1992– February 2002
20–29	–18.8	+15.7	+26.2
30–39	–10.7	+18.4	+18.1
40–49	–0.3	+14.6	+12.5
50+	+6.8	+34.8	+41.5

SOURCE: Office of Research, U.S. Department of State (10/91, 10/92, and 7/01 data), and Gallup Korea (2/02 data).

As shown, by choosing different starting and ending points, one can either demonstrate a either a decline in unfavorable sentiment (if one chooses October 1991–July 2001 as the points of comparison), or an increase (if one chooses either of the other two start and end dates), and this result holds not just for the "386 generation" but for other age groups as well.

The implication of these results is that it is impossible to draw any broader conclusions about whether South Koreans' attitudes toward the U.S. typically mellow as they get older; no robust findings appear possible from these data, as the poll-to-poll variability tends to dominate the result.

Education

Another frequently identified characteristic associated with favorable and unfavorable opinions of the U.S. is educational attainment: across a wide range of questions, we consistently found important differences by education level, and these differences were quite apparent at a fairly early age.

Figure 4.11 presents the results of a question asked of 13-to-18-year-old Koreans by Gallup Korea in 1991, broken out by their year in school, and Figure 4.12

---

[50]As we are now in the year 2003, it may be that this generation will be referred to as the "486 generation"; even democracy activists grow old.

reports the result of a question asked by Gallup Korea in April 1993 of university students by their year in school and program of study.[51]

As shown, the percentage citing the U.S. as the most-liked country falls, and the percentage citing the U.S. as the most-disliked country rises, with each year of schooling. We were unable to find any other more recent surveys of Korean youth that might have enabled us to cross-validate this finding, but as can be seen, the result is quite dramatic, leading us to wonder whether this was evidence of some sort of structural source of anti-American sentiment inherent in the Korean educational system, or the manifestation of many diffuse influences in Korean youths' social milieus, without any structural source, per se.[52]

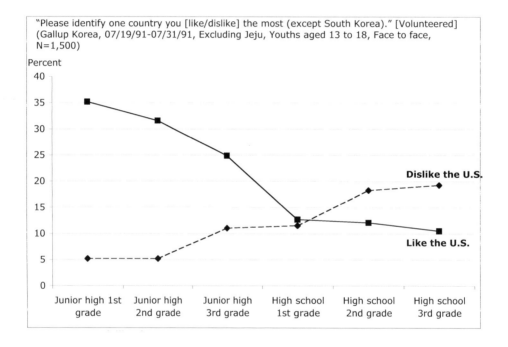

Figure 4.11—Percentage Liking and Disliking the U.S. by Education, July 1991

_____

[51]Because the poll was reported without any additional information on the number of respondents in various subgroups, in neither case were we able to conduct a Chi-square test of independence.

[52]To be clear, our research does *not* suggest that we have found conclusive evidence that South Korea's educational system is the Korean equivalent of an Islamic Madrasa in terms of its impact on attitudes toward the U.S. Although the evidence is broadly *consistent* with that explanation, it also is consistent with other explanations, and additional research is needed to better understand the reasons for the declines in favorable sentiment as Korean youth age, including the respective roles of the educational system, the media, popular culture, and other potential sources of anti-American sentiment.

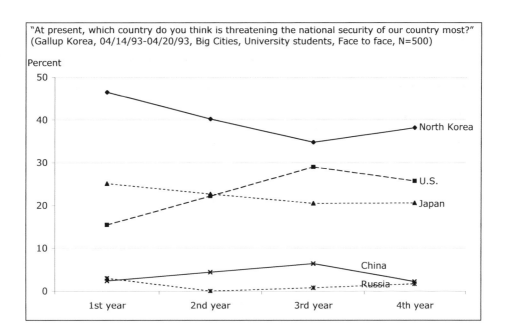

Figure 4.12—Countries Identified by University Students as the Greatest Threat, April 1993

Figure 4.12, which presents the results of a poll of university students that asked which country was the most threatening to South Korean security, suggests further erosion over young South Koreans' university career: the percentages mentioning North Korea as the greatest threat decline, while the percentages mentioning the U.S. increase, for the first three years, and then slightly reverse course.[53] Not shown, students in liberal arts programs have slightly less favorable attitudes toward the U.S. than those in science programs: whereas 25 percent of the liberal arts students thought that the U.S. was the greater threat, 21 percent of the science students felt this way.[54]

Moreover, the relationship between educational attainment and favorable attitudes toward the U.S. holds for adults as well: those who are better-educated are more likely to hold unfavorable attitudes toward the U.S. than those who are less well-educated (Figures 4.13 and 4.14).[55]

---

[53]We lacked the information on subgroup sizes necessary to conduct a Chi-square test of independence.

[54]The difference between liberal arts and science students on the threat from the north was even greater: 46 percent of the science students identified North Korea as the greatest threat, whereas only 34 percent of the liberal arts students did so.

[55]This relationship is partly complicated by age, as older South Koreans are generally less well-educated than younger ones.

98

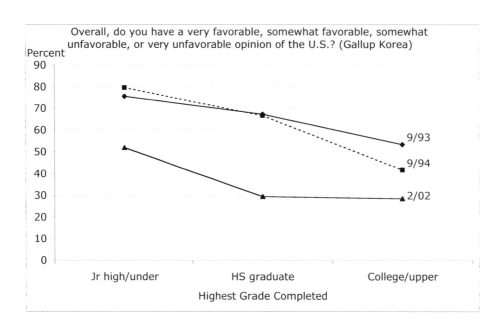

Overall, do you have a very favorable, somewhat favorable, somewhat unfavorable, or very unfavorable opinion of the U.S.? (Gallup Korea)

Figure 4.13—Percentage Favorable by Education, 9/93, 9/94, and 2/03 (Gallup Korea)

The figures show the results of three surveys by Gallup Korea: Figure 4.13 shows that the percentage with a favorable opinion of the U.S. declines and Figure 4.14 shows that the percentage with an unfavorable opinion increases—both in ways that are systematically associated with educational attainment. The results of Chi-square tests of independence were statistically significant in all three cases.[56]

Student Status

Finally, given that younger and better-educated South Koreans have less favorable views than older and less-well-educated ones, it should be no surprise that university students are among those with the least favorable views of all: a consistent finding was that those with the occupational category of student typically had among the least favorable views of the U.S.[57]

---

[56]The Chi-square test of independence revealed that all three results were statistically significant at the .001 level.

[57]The public opinion data did not really enable us to probe differences among university students, e.g., those who attend more or less prestigious universities, who majored in different fields, who were members of different social or political groups (e.g., Hanchongryon, the South Korean Federation of University Student Councils, a pro-DPRK student group), and so on.

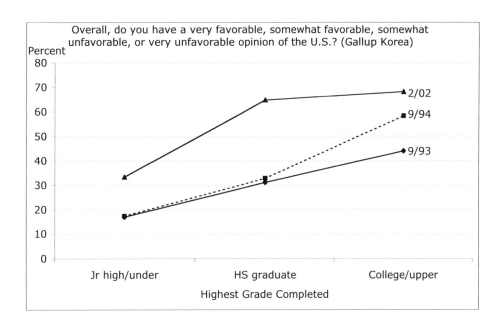

Figure 4.14—Percentage Unfavorable by Education, 9/93, 9/94, and 2/03 (Gallup Korea)

Media Consumption

Another important "filter"—but one we had no ability to model—has to do with differences in individuals' interest in politics, the amount of information they seek out on these matters, and which information channels they rely upon.[58]

Individuals typically exhibit what is called "bounded rationality"—rationality, but only in the context of the information they have available to them.[59] Thus, another potentially important individual-level factor is the extent to which South Koreans differ in the amount of information about politics and policy matters that they seek out, and which information channels they are drawn to for politically and policy-relevant relevant news. Those who seek out more information generally will be more knowledgeable about the issue, but only in the context of the range of information sources they consider.[60] Individuals also "self-select" the media sources that are compatible with preexisting beliefs.

---

[58]Scholars of American public opinion have shown that media consumption is associated with education. See Zaller (1992).

[59]In decisionmaking theory, bounded rationality also considers the limited time and other resources individuals have available in making decisions.

[60]Thus, a dedicated leftist may be drawn only to news sources that interpret the news from a leftist perspective, and a dedicated conservative may be drawn only to news sources that comport with his or her political or ideological predilections.

According to data from the Korea Press Foundation, the average South Korean spends about five hours a day in media consumption activities (Figure 4.15).[61]

Although Koreans typically rely on a variety of media information sources, they most often turn to television, radio, and newspapers,[62] but with a growing tendency toward reliance upon the Internet; South Korea has one of the highest rates of Internet penetration in the world.[63]

Korean media reporting often tends to be imbued with a strong nationalistic and even sensationalistic flavor. Moreover, many of the basic standards for objectivity, dispassionate reporting, fact-checking, and other tenets of journalism that are taken for granted in the U.S. often are not at all apparent in the Korean media.

Although there do not appear to be any actual analyses of the matter, one result may well be a general propensity for some media reporting to further inflame public sentiment by means of positive and negative messages or by their framing of events. South Koreans' heavy reliance on the visual imagery and sound bites of television news, coupled with the media's general propensity for nationalistic or sensationalistic reporting, is a potentially volatile mix.

South Koreans are aware of some of the less flattering characteristics of their media organizations, and they appear to judge the credibility of newspapers and TV reporting with a measure of skepticism (see Figure 4.16).

When judging the credibility of news organizations on a five-point scale, where one means "not at all confident" and five means "very confident," South Koreans typically have rated the credibility of their newspapers and television broadcasts as only slightly better than a three. Also shown, with the exception of the first and last data points, the credibility ratings for the two media generally have moved together. Since about 1996, however, the credibility of broadcast

---

[61]It seems likely that some multi-tasking in fact may be going on, e.g., listening to the radio at work, and watching television or listening to the radio while on line, so the estimate of five hours per day may be somewhat exaggerated.

[62]On average, somewhere between 20-40 percent of South Koreans read newspapers daily. A 1996 estimate from the ROK's National Statistical Office suggested that 40.6 percent of those 15 years old and over read the paper every day. See http://www.kpf.or.kr/english/facts_2001_03.html......... The country's newspaper readership was estimated at 200 out of every 1,000 people in a recent report authored by the Korea Newpapers Association and Professor Lee Mi-young of Yonsei University. See Yonhap, October 22, 2003.

[63]A recent survey by Ipsos-Insight found that 70 percent of the South Korean adult population had used the Internet in the past 30 days, and estimated the user population at 23 million. While Canada had a comparably high rate of Internet use (71 percent), South Korean adult Internet use was higher than that in the U.S., Japan, Germany, the United Kingdom, France, or any of the other populations surveyed. See Ipsos-Insight (2004).

television reporting has surpassed that of the newspapers, largely attributable to a decline in the credibility of newspaper reporting.

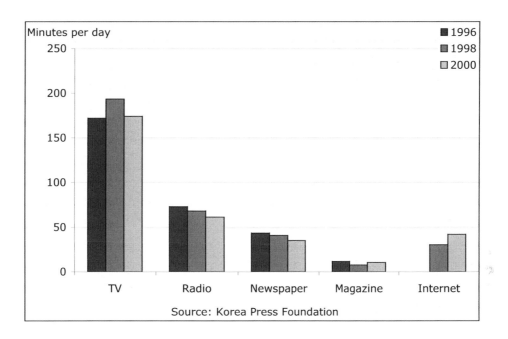

Figure 4.15—Korean Average Daily Media Consumption, 1996–2000

Figure 4.16—Credibility of Newspaper and Television Broadcast Media

In light of these doubts about the news they receive from mainstream sources, it should be little surprise that many South Koreans—especially young Koreans and students—increasingly turn to alternative news sources (Table 4.13).[64]

Table 4.13

Main Media Source for News, September 2003

What form of media do you usually get your news from? Tell me the most influential media channel for you

Age	TV	Newspaper	Radio	Magazines	Internet
20s	75.9%	6.2%	0%	0.7%	17.2%
30s	80.6	15.5	0	0	3.9
40s	77.8	16.8	2	0	3.5
50+	81.0	16.8	1.7	0	0.5
Students	74.2	2	0	2	21.8
All	78.9%	13.8%	0.8%	0.2%	6.2%

SOURCE: *JoongAng Ilbo*-CSIS-RAND survey, September 15–17, 2003, N=1,000.

As shown in the table, the media consumption habits of the 20-somethings and students stand out in a number of ways.[65] Most obviously, younger Koreans and students are four to five times more likely to depend on the Internet as their primary source of news than the other age groups. Younger South Koreans and students also are less than half as likely to rely on a daily newspaper for their news, and they are the greatest consumers of special interest and other magazines as their primary source of news. These data suggest that many younger South Koreans and students have moved away from mainstream news sources and instead are opting for a different mix of news sources than the average South Korean, and perhaps leading to a distinct set of political and social views that also differ from mainstream Korean society.

In seeking information on the Internet, Koreans can choose from a wide number of websites offering news. These include official sources such as Korea's government ministries; official news organizations, such as Yonhap and its affiliated broadcast outlets; online editions of major newspapers, magazines, and

---

[64]According to the Korea Press Foundation, a majority of South Koreans surveyed identify the Internet as the media outlet of choice to obtain specialized information.

[65]For a recent analysis of American media consumption habits that also finds younger Americans turning to alternative information sources, see Pew Research Center (2004).

broadcast outlets; independent news outlets such as OhMyNews;[66] and websites maintained by a variety of nongovernmental organizations and private persons. And the cost of finding the news of greatest interest can be fairly low relative to other sources—the equivalent of clicking on a hot link or entering search terms in a search engine.

There also is anecdotal evidence to suggest that younger South Koreans receive a higher percentage of their information from Internet news web sites like OhMyNews which are far more critical of the U.S. than the mainstream media.[67] There also is at least some evidence that at least some students and younger South Koreans are frequent visitors of dissident and anti-American web sites (see Table 4.14).

The table presents the results of an online survey regarding continuation of the candlelight vigils that was posted at the website of Pomdaewi, an organization created in the wake of the June 2002 deaths of the schoolgirls to allow for the exchange of views and to organize candlelight vigils and other expressions of anti-American sentiment.[68]

As shown in the table, those taking an online survey regarding continuation of the candlelight vigils in January 2003 were primarily male, young, and students, but respondents also included substantial percentages of professionals and office workers. While those who took the online survey certainly were not representative of South Korean society at large—compare the demographics of the respondents with those for the larger population—they may be quite representative of those who are most inclined to anti-American expressions.

A possible result is that the young, students, and the better-educated—precisely the demographics of those who are the principal users of the Internet and those who consistently express the least favorable views of the U.S.—will develop an

---

[66]The avowed aim of OhMyNews is to balance media coverage by actively offsetting what it sees as a largely conservative, mainstream media. Its motto is" every citizen is a potential reporter." See French (2003).

[67]According to GNP party leader Choe Byung-yul, "Some 47 percent of the eligible voters in their 20's and 30's no longer read newspapers." Mr. Choe spoke at a forum hosted by the Kwanhun Club, a fraternity of senior journalists. T'ae-kyong (2003).

[68]Pomdaewi is the Pan-National Countermeasure Committee for the U.S. Military Armored Vehicle's Murder of the Late Middle School Girls Sin-Hyo-sun and Sim Mi-son.

Table 4.14

Demographics of Online Survey at Pomdaewi Dissident Website

	Poll	Est. 2000 Population
Gender:*		
Female	31%	50.3%
Male	59	49.7
Age:		
20 years or younger	26%	29.3%
21–25 years	19	8.3
26–30 years	20	9.2
31–35 years	19	9.1
36–40 years	9	8.9
41–45 years	5	8.6
46–50 years	2	6.5
50 years or older	1	20.0
Occupation:		
Student (High school or below)	24%	na
College student (Graduate students included)	21	na
Laborer	6	na
Farmer	1	na
Office worker	13	na
Professional	14	na
Housewife	2	na
Administrative	6	na
Artist	2	na
Other	12	na

NOTE: Pomdaewi (Pan-National Countermeasure Committee for the U.S. Military Armored Vehicle's Murder of the Late Middle School Girls Sin-Hyo-sun and Sim Mi-son website, at <http://www.antimigun.org>, accessed January 7, 2003. Total number of respondents was 4,233 as of the conclusion of the survey at 1000 local time on January 7, 2003. * = Numbers as reported do not add to 100 percent. na = not applicable. Population data from U.S. Census Bureau's International Data Base (IDB), July 2003 version, online at http://www.census.gov/ipc/www/idbsum.html, accessed February 2004.

increasingly intemperate and unpredictable set of views toward the U.S., increasingly straying from the more temperate views of the ROK government and South Korean society at large.

Indeed, the data from the Pomdaewi online poll suggests that large percentages of those who took the survey not only were inclined to resist South Korean leaders' calls to end the candlelight vigils, but also held rather hardened attitudes about how far they were willing to go to demonstrate (Table 4.15); unfortunately, we did not find any contemporaneous polling of the total adult population on this subject, and so cannot establish the extent these views diverged from those of the average South Korean.

Table 4.15

Online Survey at Dissident Website: Attitudes Toward Arresting Pomdaewi

What do you, as a netizen, think about some netizens' call to halt the peaceful candlelight vigils?

	Percent
Since we have ROK-US relations, we should stop the candlelight demonstrations immediately	12
We cannot stop the candlelight vigils without a resolution to the Hyo-sun and Mi-son issue	88

What should be done in an instance when police obstruct peaceful marches?

	Percent
Voluntarily disperse	9
Protest and voluntarily disperse	21
Definitely carry out the march using peaceful methods	4
Protest and request that they move	7
Protest and fight with them, etc.	59

NOTE: Pomdaewi (Pan-National Countermeasure Committee for the U.S. Military Armored Vehicle's Murder of the Late Middle School Girls Sin-Hyo-sun and Sim Mi-son website, at http://www.antimigun.org, accessed January 7, 2003. Total number of respondents was 4,233 as of the conclusion of the survey at 1000 local time on January 7, 2003.

To conclude, Koreans have many sources to choose from in the saturated information markets of Korea, and there is at least some evidence that those who are most inclined to have unfavorable views of the U.S. also are those who are turning from mainstream news sources to alternative sources. And given that the Internet serves these Koreans as both an information source and a tool for mass mobilization, the result may well be greater difficulties in managing the most virulent forms of anti-American sentiment.

Nationalism

As described in Chapter 2, events that hit the nerve of South Korean nationalism and sovereignty can lead to particularly strong reactions.[69] We were able to identify three questions that enabled us to somewhat better understand the relationship between nationalism and favorable or unfavorable attitudes toward the U.S.

---

[69]Donald Clark has suggested that some anti-Americanism is a "mirror of Korean pride." See Clark (1991), p. 157.

Our first indicator of nationalism was a question from the Pew Research Center that asked respondents whether they thought the U.S. took into account the interests of other nations like South Korea in its international policy decisions (Table 4.16). We reasoned that the belief that the U.S. did not would be most strongly held by those who were most fervent about protecting South Korea's sovereignty and independence, and most desirous of equal treatment in the bilateral relationship. We used the Chi-square test of independence to assess the relationship between favorable sentiment and the belief that the U.S. takes into account South Korea's interests in its decisionmaking.

Table 4.16

**Cross-Tabulation of Attitude Toward U.S. and Belief That U.S. Takes Other Nations'
Interests into Account**

Sentiment Toward U.S.	Extent to Which U.S. Takes Into Account South Korean Interests				
	Great Deal	Fair Amount	Not Too Much	Not At All	DK/Ref
Very favorable	15%	8%	3%	3%	7%
Somewhat favorable	50	63	51	27	45
Somewhat unfavorable	23	25	38	52	42
Very unfavorable	6	4	5	15	3
DK/Refused	6	1	3	3	3
All	5%	18%	54%	19	4
			p-value for Chi-square test:		<.001

Source: Pew Research Center Global Attitudes Survey, July–August 2002.
NOTE: Question wordings were as follows: "Please tell me if you have a very favorable, somewhat favorable, somewhat unfavorable or very unfavorable opinion of the United States" and "In making international policy decisions, to what extent do you think the United States takes into account the interests of countries like (survey country)—a great deal, a fair amount, not too much or not at all?"

As expected, the stronger the belief that the U.S. took other nations' interests into account, the greater the likelihood of holding a favorable view of the U.S.; this result also was statistically significant. Given that fewer than one in four South Koreans believe that the U.S. takes other nations interests into account, however, this belief can be seen to be an important potential source of unfavorable sentiment toward the U.S.

As a second test of the relationship between South Korean nationalism and favorable and unfavorable sentiment toward the U.S., we cross-tabulated another question from the Pew Research Center that asked respondents if they felt that their culture was superior to others with the standard question on attitudes toward the U.S. We reasoned that those with the strongest belief that South

Korean culture was superior would also be those with the least favorable attitudes.

As shown in Table 4.17, the Chi-square test of independence suggested a statistically significant relationship between the two variables, but the relationship in fact was in the opposite direction of our hypothesis.

Table 4.17

Cross-Tabulation of Favorable Attitude and Belief That Culture Is Superior

| Sentiment Toward U.S. | Belief That Korean Culture Is Superior to Others | | | | |
	Completely Agree	Mostly Agree	Mostly Disagree	Completely Disagree	DK Refused
Very favorable	6%	3%	4%	0%	14%
Somewhat favorable	46	52	41	14	29
Somewhat unfavorable	35	38	46	29	29
Very unfavorable	10	5	9	29	14
DK/Refused	3	2	0	29	14
All	33%	57%	7%	1%	2%

p-value for Chi-square test: <.001

Source: Pew Research Center Global Attitudes Survey, July-August 2002.
NOTE: Question wordings were as follows: "Please tell me if you have a very favorable, somewhat favorable, somewhat unfavorable or very unfavorable opinion of the United States" and "Here is a list of statements. For each one, please tell me whether you completely agree, mostly agree, mostly disagree or completely disagree with it. [SHOW CARD]…Our people are not perfect, but our culture is superior to others"

Thus, the data were consistent with a very different explanation: a favorable attitude toward the U.S. is in fact associated with South Koreans' level of security about the superiority of their culture. Specifically, the more insecure South Koreans are about the superiority of Korean culture, the less favorable they are toward the U.S.; the more secure they are about Korean culture, the more favorable their opinions are toward the U.S. This association between insecurity and unfavorable sentiment has some resonance with the explanations in Tables 4.4 and 4.5 that South Koreans themselves gave as the main reasons that some dislike the U.S., especially the U.S.'s power and wealth and the belief that Americans look down on Koreans.

Our third indicator of nationalism comes from the U.S. Department of State's polling before and after the June 2000 North-South summit, at a time when South Korean national pride was peaking (see Table 4.18).[70]

Table 4.18

Attitudes Toward U.S., China, and Japan Before and After June 2000 Korean Summit

	Before May 2000	After September 2000
United States	71%	58%
China	72	56
Japan	44	35

Source: Office of Research, U.S. Department of State.

As shown in the table, the State Department polled one month before the summit and three months after it. Not only did favorable sentiment toward the U.S. decline between these readings, but favorable sentiment toward China and Japan declined as well.[71] Although this evidence cannot prove that the decline in favorable sentiment toward all three countries was attributable to swelling South Korean nationalism, the result is certainly consistent with that interpretation.

A Modest Role for Regionalism

Although much in South Korean politics is colored by regionalism and there are places in South Korea where anti-American sentiment seems to flare readily (e.g., Kwangju and Jeolla provinces), geography does not appear to have a particularly important impact on favorable and unfavorable views toward the U.S.

Table 4.19 presents data on sentiment toward the U.S. by city and province from three Gallup Korea polls conducted over the last decade.[72]

---

[70] The authors thank James Marshall of the Office of Research, U.S. Department of State, for bringing this to our attention.

[71] The authors are grateful to James Marshall of the U.S. Department of State's Office of Research for bringing this to our attention.

[72] In two surveys, Gallup Korea combined the two Chungcheong provinces, the two Geongsang provinces, and the two Jeolla provinces. It is worth mentioning, however, that there were significant differences in the February 2003 between the northern and southern provinces.

Table 4.19

**Attitudes Toward the U.S. by Geography,
September 1993, September 1994, and February 2002**

Political Unit	% FAVORABLE			% UNFAVORABLE		
	Sep-93	Sep-94	Feb-02	Sep-93	Sep-94	Feb-02
Seoul	63.2	61.3	35.2	32.9	38.7	58.5
Busan	71.0	58.3	38.9	22.9	39.3	59.5
Daegu	56.4	66.7	34.4	41.9	33.3	56.9
Gwangju	68.7	50.6	20.0	28.5	49.4	80.0
Big cities	64.5	61.1	33.0	32.1	38.4	61.6
Middle & small cities	66.9	55.8	32.1	30.1	42.1	60.1
Other cities	66.5	57.6	na	31.1	40.8	na
Eup/Myon (towns)	69.6	78.7	40.7	25.2	19.7	51.4
Provinces	69.6	78.7	na	25.2	19.7	na
Chungcheong	78.1	66.0	na	21.9	34.1	na
Gangwon	46.7	74.7	25.6	49.5	25.3	74.4
Gyeonggi	64.9	61.4	29.8	33.4	37.8	62.8
Gyeongsang	71.3	66.3	na	21.3	31.2	na
Jeolla	62.4	61.3	na	36.9	36.3	na

SOURCE: Gallup Korea, 9/93, 9/94, and 2/02.

To assess the importance of geographic factors in attitudes toward the U.S. over time, we calculated the between-survey correlations for the cities, provinces, and other political units listed in the table.[73] The modest correlations that resulted suggested that geography plays only a modest role in shaping attitudes toward the U.S, at best accounting for perhaps only 15 percent of the variance in favorable and unfavorable sentiment.[74]

Societal Influences

We now turn to a number of broader societal influences that appear to be important in shaping South Koreans' attitudes toward the U.S.

---

[73]The hypothesis we were testing was that differences between the geographic units would tend to dominate any changes that might occur over time.

[74]The correlations between surveys for favorable attitudes ranged from –0.17 to 0.40, and the correlations between surveys for unfavorable attitudes ranged from -0.03 to 0.42. Thus, at best, geography can explain about 16 percent of the variance in a simple regression of favorable or unfavorable sentiment on geographic unit, and probably less, given that our multivariate statistical modeling is able to do such a good job predicting favorable and unfavorable sentiment even without geography included. Clearly, further research is indicated on the importance of geography relative to other explanatory variables.

Leadership

Opinion Leadership by Government Leaders

Chapter 2 described a number of instances in which South Korean political leaders made statements or took actions to influence attitudes and behavior toward the U.S., and our advisory group averred the importance of leadership in helping to shape attitudes toward the U.S.

Numerous episodes suggest that such efforts vary in their effectiveness in influencing South Koreans' attitudes and actions toward the U.S.: President Kim Dae Jung's efforts to limit expressions of anti-American sentiment at the June 2002 World Cup,[75] and Prime Minister Koh Kun's warning in June 2003 not to let the anniversary of the schoolgirls' deaths lead to another round of candlelight vigils and other anti-American expression appear to have been successful, whereas various leaders' efforts to bring an end to the candlelight vigils in December 2002[76] and President Roh's warning to Chongyojo, a progressive teacher's group, against giving "anti-American lessons" to their students, may have had only limited effect.[77]

In spite of the mixed track record for these efforts, the record suggests the importance of South Korean leaders making a conscious effort to influence attitudes in ways that foster a more favorable opinion environment for the U.S.-South Korean bilateral relationship, and the presence of U.S. forces.

Next-Generation Leaders

Another form of leadership is opinion leadership by the next generation of elites, i.e., the avant garde in any political society. The available data present a worrisome picture in this regard: next-generation South Korean leaders appear to hold a set of beliefs that are much less favorable toward the U.S., and as they continue to take positions of greater responsibility and higher public profile, their opinions can be expected to influence mass opinion.[78]

---

[75]See "ROK President Calls on Soccer Fans for 'Decent' Behavior During ROK-U.S. Match," *The Korea Times*, June 8, 2002, and "Official Says ROKG Not 'Seriously' Concerned About 'Eruption' of Anti-American Sentiment on 10 June," *The Korea Times*, June 6, 2002.

[76]See "ROK President-Elect Calls for End to Anti-U.S. Candlelight Vigils," Yonhap, December 28, 2002, and "Even the President-Elect is Appealing for Restraining of Demonstrations," *Dong-A Ilbo*, December 30, 2002.

[77]Yong-chin (2003). According to this report, the teacher's group reacted angrily, and Roh added that he would not make an issue out of the content of lessons given by Chongyojo members, which are said to include anti-American materials, such as photos of the body of a Korean killed by an American soldier. "

[78]The best analysis of this issue is Watts (2002). Watts had Gallup Korea interview next-generation South Korean leaders to ascertain their attitudes toward the U.S.

As shown in Table 4.20, the small sample of next generation of South Korean leaders polled in November 2001 generally believed that the U.S. benefits more from the bilateral relationship than does South Korea, and that the principal advantage for South Korea is the additional security and, to a lesser extent, economic benefits that the relationship provides.[79]

Table 4.20

Next-Generation Leaders' Opinions on the Beneficiary of the Bilateral Relationship

"Which country do you think is the beneficiary of the US-South Korean relations?" (Potomac Associates and Gallup Korea, 11/01-12/01, Leaders of next generation aged 30 to 49, Individual interview, n=51)

Percent	Opinion
59	The United States
37	South Korea
4	Others / Don't know / Refused

"What do you think is the most important advantage that South Korea has had from the US-South Korean relations?" (Potomac Associates & Gallup Korea, 11/01-12/01, Leaders of next generation aged 30 to 49, Individual interview, n=51)

Percent	Opinion
70	National security
22	Economic advantage
8	Others / Don't know / Refused

Source: Monthly Chosun, 05/01/2002

And as shown in Table 4.21, these sentiments are echoed in the data for the mass public: a growing percentage appear to believe that the U.S. derives the greatest advantage from the presence of U.S. military forces in South Korea.

While we cannot demonstrate a cause and effect relationship, the fact the mass public opinion on the matter appears to be converging with the views of the next generation of South Korean leaders suggests a sufficient basis for concern about future mass attitudes regarding the bilateral relationship.

---

[79]Watts (2002) also found that 90 percent of the next generation of South Korean leaders that were interviewed conceived of the benefits from the bilateral relationship in terms of security or economic benefits.

The Media

As described earlier, individuals construct their worldviews in a somewhat ad hoc fashion, integrating information from various media that can differ in their focus and content. We also suggested that the nationalistic and sensationalistic nature of the Korean press could be presenting the news on the U.S. in ways that erode Koreans' favorable images of the U.S., and amplify negative sentiment.[80]

Table 4.21

The Beneficiary of the U.S. Military Forces in Korea

"Which country do you think takes advantage of the US military forces stationed in South Korea most?" (*The Hankyoreh 21*, 06/26/00, Adults aged 20 and older, n=700)

Percent	Opinion
43.0	The United States
27.9	South Korea
2.1	North Korea
3.7	Japan
20.1	China
15.4	Both the US and South Korea have some advantages
5.7	Don't know / Refused

"Which country do you think takes advantage of the US military forces stationed in South Korea most?" (*The Hankyoreh 21*, 3/8-9/02, Adults aged 20 and older, n=500)

Percent	Opinion
52.6	The United States
28.3	South Korea
19.1	Others / Don't know / Refused

Source: *The Hankyoreh 21*, 07/18/2000 and 03/12/2002.

To better understand the character of Korean media reporting, as part of our study we undertook a simple content analysis of reporting on the U.S. and North Korea from 1990 to 2002 by five of the major Korean newspapers.[81]

---

[80]Donald Clark usefully suggests: "Any public opinion about the United States in Korea, therefore, ought to be taken as an opinion about an America stereotyped by the unique terms of the Korean-American encounter. Furthermore, different Koreans have experienced Americans differently, so they do not all have the same stereotype. Instead, their attitudes are shifting combinations of several basic—and sometimes contradictory—impressions: America the Historic Helper, America the Careless Colossus, America the Ailing Giant, and America the Ruthless Hegemon." See Clark (1991), p. 151.

[81]We collected data on stories from *Chosun Ilbo, JoongAng Ilbo, Dong-A Ilbo, Hankook Ilbo*, and *The Hankyoreh* for our analysis.

Our content analysis consisted of using simple combinations of search terms (typically, "U.S." or "North Korea" combined with some other term like "U.S. Forces Korea" or "reunification"). These simple content analyses of newspaper reporting suggest that there has been a fairly substantial increase in the share of reporting devoted to the U.S., and a gradual decline in reporting both on North Korea, and on "reunification." (Figure 4.17)[82]

As shown in the figure, reporting on the U.S. as a share of total reporting rose from about 7 percent in 1990 to about 12 percent in 2002, while reporting on North Korea declined from 5 percent to about 3 percent of total reporting, and reporting on "reunification" declined from 4 to 1 percent.

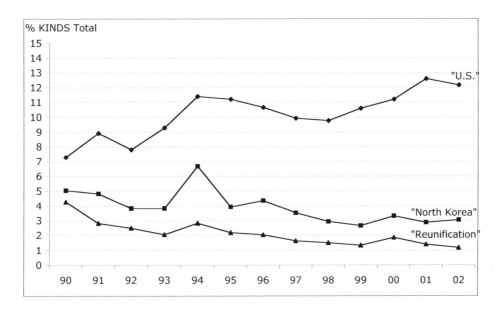

Figure 4.17—Major Korean Newspaper Reporting on the U.S., North Korea, and Reunification, 1990–2002

One interpretation of these data is that various aspects of U.S.-South Korean relations have come under much greater scrutiny by the press over the period, even as the press have become less attentive to developments related to North Korea. And the declining attention to reunification would be consistent with a long-term secular decline in optimism about reunification since the heady days of the immediate post-Cold War period.

We further broke down reporting on the U.S. and North Korea into a number of topics of interest (Figures 4.18 and 4.19).

---

[82]Our content analyses involved simple keyword searches, such as "United States."

114

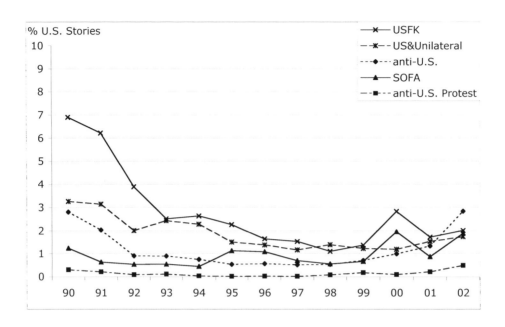

Figure 4.18—Selected Topics in Major Korean Newspaper Reporting on the U.S., 1990–2002

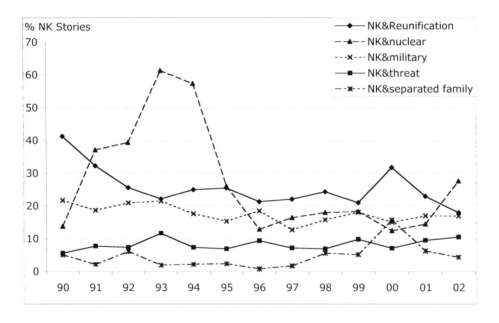

Figure 4.19—Selected Topics in Major Korean Newspaper Reporting on North Korea, 1990–2002

Recalling that the share of stories devoted to the U.S. was an increasing one over the period, as shown in Figure 4.18, the share of news stories that mentioned U.S. Forces Korea declined from about 7 percent of the total stories on the U.S. in 1990 to about 2 percent in 2002. The share of stories that mentioned U.S. unilateralism declined from a little over 3 percent to about 1-1/2 percent, and then recently climbed back to about 2 percent. The share of stories that mentioned anti-Americanism or anti-American sentiment fell from just under 3 percent to less than 1 percent, and then recovered to the 3 percent range. And the percentage of stories that mentioned the Status of Forces Agreement (SOFA) oscillated around 1 percent until the most recent period, when it approached 2 percent of total stories.

The impression one gets from these data is that topics that had perhaps the strongest potential for critical reporting on the U.S. generally constituted a very small percent of overall reporting toward the U.S., but there was a perceptible increase in such reporting in 2002, at the time of the most recent downturn in sentiment toward the U.S.[83] Moreover, given the overall increase in reporting on the U.S., the data in Figure 4.18 would understate this. It is, of course, impossible to determine how this increase in reporting might have shaped Koreans' views of the U.S. during the period (or vice-versa).[84]

Also recalling the overall declining trend in the share of major Korean newspapers' reporting devoted to North Korea over the period, we also broke the reporting on North Korea down into some sensible topical areas (Figure 4.19). The figure shows that, with the exception of the 1991–1995 period and 2002 (when reporting on nuclear developments dominated), the largest share of stories (typically 20–30 percent) mentioned reunification, but mentions of reunification declined from about 40 percent of all stories that mentioned North Korea to less than 20 percent; the spike in 2000 is no doubt attributable to the June 2000 summit between Kim Jong-Il and Kim Dae Jung.

There also was a slight decline in reporting that mentioned North Korea and "military" within a narrow (25–30 percent range), and a slight increase in reporting that mentioned North Korea and "threat," within an equally narrow (5-10 percent) range. Stories mentioning separated families hovered below 5 percent of North Korea-related stories until about 1998, peaked in 2000 (the issue was a key topic of discussion in the June 2000 summit), and then fell again.

---

[83]If we sum the percentages devoted to these topics, the total percentage rises from 5.7 percent in 2001 to nine percent in 2002. This does not account for possible double-counting of stories, however.

[84]Readership interests also shape editorial decisions regarding topic coverage. It is worth mentioning that most of the reporting on anti-Americanism probably is reporting *on* anti-Americanism, not necessarily its promotion.

These data suggest a mixture of hope and fear in newspapers' reporting on North Korea: hope for reunification and the reunion of separated families, coupled with fear of the north's nuclear and conventional military capabilities.

The Korean Educational System

Finally, we return to the issue of education as a source of unfavorable attitudes toward the U.S. We earlier presented data that showed increasingly unfavorable attitudes for middle school and high school students (Figure 4.11) and for university students (Figure 4.12), and showed that educational attainment generally was associated with favorable and unfavorable attitudes toward the U.S. among adults as well (Figures 4.13 and 4.14).

There is, moreover, anecdotal evidence of anti-American content in teaching curricula especially those used by the Korea Teachers and Educational Workers Union, a progressive and pro-north labor union that seems to have been given a relatively free hand to use anti-American propaganda in their teaching materials. As shown in the box on the next page, students could fail a pop quiz on the recent Iraq war if they failed to choose the incorrect answer from a number of highly tendentious choices.

While the available data do not allow us either to reject or confirm the hypothesis that the South Korean public school and university systems may constitute another source of anti-American sentiment[85]—and we are decidedly not arguing that the South Korean educational system constitutes the Korean equivalent of an Islamic madrasa—the available empirical and anecdotal evidence is certainly consistent with the proposition that it may be playing a role in fostering less favorable attitudes toward the U.S.[86] Whether or not the Korean educational system comprises a structural source of anti-American sentiment is well beyond the scope of the present study, but the evidence suggests that is a subject that is deserving of its own in-depth analysis.

---

[85]Put another way, the fact that we were unable to reject the hypothesis does not necessarily mean that it is true.

[86]It also is consistent, however, with the proposition that as young South Koreans become politically socialized, an increasingly critical view of the U.S. is a part of that socialization, and that young adults and the better educated have the greatest influence on young South Koreans. To establish any causal relationship, one would want to conduct panel survey of young South Koreans over their entire educational careers; to the authors' knowledge, no such effort currently exists.

Korea Teachers and Educational Workers Union Quiz on the Iraq War

Which of the following descriptions of America is incorrect:

(1) The world's leading arms-exporting country.

(2) The world's most heavily nuclear-armed country.

(3) The world's leader in chemical weapons research.

(4) The world's most peace-loving country that never once was at war with other countries.*

Which of the following descriptions of Iraq after the Gulf War is incorrect?

(1) Due to economic sanctions, infant mortality increased by 150%, and in some areas, 70% of newborns had leukemia.

(2) The United States and Britain conducted a bombing campaign against Iraq for 11 years after the war, causing terror among the Iraqi people.

(3) Cancer among Iraqi children increased by 700% because of depleted uranium left from the bombing.

(4) The infant mortality rate of Iraqi children in 1999 was 300% higher than it was a decade earlier.

(5) Not a single Iraqi starved to death after the Gulf War because of the extensive food relief program.*

Quiz questions included in supplemental teaching package on the war in Iraq distributed in March 2003 by the Korea Teachers and Educational Workers Union given to about 400,000 South Korean Students, as reported in Barbara Demick, "U.S. Gets a Bad Name in South Korean Schools," *Los Angeles Times*, July 12, 2003. Correct responses are denoted by an asterisk (*).

Popular Culture

To be complete, there also is some anecdotal evidence of anti-American strains in South Korean popular culture, especially youth culture, although it is hard to get a sense of its prevalence and consequence.[87]

We earlier cited an underground pop hit, the lyrics of which express a great deal of pent-up hostility toward the U.S.,[88] and also noted a South Korean pop music video from about the same period (just after the Ohno skating incident) that showed the band members humiliating Americans, and was said to be quite popular among younger South Koreans. There also is anecdotal evidence that many of the South Korean films that are most popular to young South Koreans increasingly are portraying North Koreans in a more favorable light, and portraying Americans as murderers and evil schemers.[89] Taken together, these are areas that bear watching, as they also could well influence the youngest South Koreans' future attitudes toward the U.S.

Chapter Conclusions

This chapter has explored a wide range of potential sources for South Koreans' favorable and unfavorable opinions toward the U.S., both at the individual level and at the societal level, and has shown that, like sentiment toward the U.S. itself, the sources of attitudes toward the U.S. are varied and their effects and interactions quite complex: The Korean notions of *panmi* (anti-Americanism) and *pimi* (criticizing the U.S.) mask the breadth, depth, and patterns of unfavorable orientations toward the U.S., and a more sophisticated conceptualization of orientations toward the U.S. as a multi-dimensional and multi-level phenomenon is needed.[90]

---

[87]To our knowledge, there have been no content analyses of Korean music, films, television, or other media that could provide an empirical understanding of its prevalence.

[88]An excerpt of the lyrics includes: "So now we are shouting "Yankee, go home" / Yankee, you will pay for this after our reunification / Grand country, the reunified Korea / We will reunify the country / By the power of the Korean people / Grand country, the reunified Korea / Don't forget the blood-stained history of Korea! / You ringleader of Korea's division, f***ing U.S.A. / Don't forget the Nogun-ri massacre of civilians! / You country of murderers, f***ing U.S.A. "F***ing U.S.A.," lyrics by Yoon Min-sok.

[89]According to one report, since the advent of Sunshine Policy, the role of devil has more often been reserved for Americans than North Koreans. See Brooke (2002). The authors wish to thank Larry Diamond of the Hoover Institution for bringing this to our attention. Donald Clark notes that "[m]otion pictures have always presented Koreans with their most powerful images of America." See Donald N. Clark (1991), p. 150.

[90]We are indebted to one of our advisory group members, Professor Doh C. Shin for this point, who also suggested that the literature of attitudinal dynamics would appear to offer a powerful foundation for future analyses of the issues discussed in this report.

We showed that South Koreans' attitudes toward the U.S. were systematically associated with beliefs about the state of U.S.-South Korean relations and the importance of U.S. forces for protecting South Korea's security, and explained that our statistical modeling suggested that these two beliefs were very good predictors of overall sentiment toward the U.S.

This may help to explain why there has only been a partial recovery in overall attitudes toward the U.S.: according to our most recent reading of attitudes regarding the health of the bilateral relationship (from the September 2003 *JoonAng Ilbo*-CSIS-RAND poll that was developed in cooperation with RAND), only about one in three thought that the relationship was in good shape; continued doubts about the bilateral relationship may be creating drag—or even stalling—a complete recovery in favorable sentiment toward the U.S.

We also showed that the perceived importance of U.S. forces could be predicted from beliefs about the threat from the north, the regional military balance, and the credibility of the U.S. commitment; we conjectured that beliefs about the prospects for reunification also are an important predictor. We also demonstrated that a number of individual-level characteristics—age, education, and student status—are important lenses on attitudes toward the U.S.; when included in our multivariate models, these factors somewhat improved our overall predictions of individual-level favorable or unfavorable sentiment.

As also shown, South Korean nationalism plays out in both predictable and somewhat unpredictable ways: The belief that the U.S. does not take into account South Korea's interests was associated somewhat predictably with less-favorable attitudes toward the U.S., but the belief that South Korean culture was superior was unexpectedly associated with more-favorable attitudes.

Based upon three polls conducted over about a decade, we also unexpectedly discovered that regionalism appears to play only a modest role in explaining favorable and unfavorable sentiment toward the U.S., at least relative to events and other factors. Finally, we offered some conjectures on potential additional influences, the direction and strength of which were impossible for us to quantify: the roles of leadership, the media, the Korean educational system, and Korean popular (and especially youth) culture. These would be excellent areas for further research.

In the next chapter, we turn to the implications of this work and offer recommendations for U.S. policymakers.

5. Implications, Recommendations, Conclusions

Implications for the U.S.

The public opinion data suggest that we may have weathered the most recent downturn in U.S.-South Korean relations, a downturn that came during a generally favorable period in which positive sentiment toward the U.S. had, for the most part, been strong and on the rise. This downturn appears to have been relatively short-lived, and, as of the fall of 2003, a recovery appears to be in progress. Whether a full recovery in favorable sentiment toward the U.S. actually will result remains uncertain: There are many easily imaginable developments that could reverse the trend, but there are ample reasons for cautious optimism.

In the short term, Korean attitudes could well improve further, for a number of reasons. President Roh's favorable treatment of the U.S. and the alliance since the spring of 2003 may diminish the propensity of some of his constituency to engage in expressions of anti-American sentiment. ROK involvement as a full partner in the six-party talks on the North Korean nuclear program could help to diminish sensitivities about the subordination of Korean interests, and improve perceptions of U.S.-ROK relations as being balanced and equitable. North Korean saber-rattling over its nuclear weapons program would be expected to raise concerns about the threat from the north, enhance the perceived importance of the U.S.'s historical role in helping to secure South Korea's security, and buoy favorable sentiment toward the U.S. Finally, the restructuring and relocation of U.S. forces could help to alleviate many of the base-related strains that constitute a recurring source of friction in U.S.-South Korean relations.

Still, this is no time for complacency about South Korean views of the U.S. and the bilateral relationship. Despite the efforts of U.S. and South Korean policymakers to put bilateral relations back on track, there has as yet been only a partial recovery in favorable sentiment toward the U.S. This seems to be attributable to the continued, widespread belief that the bilateral relationship is in poor shape, which appears to be placing drag on a full recovery. Whether a recovery in favorable sentiment has temporarily stalled, we are at some sort of "tipping point," or attitudes have stabilized at a new, lower level cannot be known at this point. But the issue begs policy attention from both the U.S. and South Korea.

The challenge of dealing with North Korea most likely will continue to test the alliance, as South Korea seeks to balance its two-track policy regarding inter-Korean affairs and the nuclear problem in the north, and as Pyongyang continues its efforts to create or exploit divisions between the U.S. and South Korea; there are many opportunities for miscalculation and missteps in the U.S.-ROK-DPRK *pas-de-trois* that could lead to friction in the alliance, and heightened ambivalence within the South Korean public. Fostering favorable South Korean media reporting and public attitudes toward the Future of the Alliance initiative, for example, could continue to be a challenge.

Moreover, although many specific U.S. policies appear to be implicated in anti-American sentiment in South Korea, some unfavorable attitudes appear to transcend the current U.S. administration. The U.S.'s global war on terrorism and its efforts to prevent proliferation of weapons of mass destruction, for example, frames North Korea in a way that is very different from South Korea's views of the north, and these differences seem likely to persist in form, if not degree.

South Korea's development of an "independent national defense"—a policy encouraged by the U.S.—also could lead to declines in favorable sentiment toward the U.S. All else equal, such a development likely would result in the belief that the local military balance on the peninsula had improved, and that the need for U.S. forces and the alliance had accordingly diminished. Given that beliefs about the importance of U.S. forces are a key predictor of favorable opinion, the result could be further erosion in favorable sentiment toward the U.S. The same line of reasoning would apply if the North Korean threat were to diminish, or vanish.

And as described in this report, younger cohorts have much less favorable attitudes than their parents, and better-educated South Koreans generally have less favorable attitudes than less well-educated ones. While the data cannot as yet be used to support an argument of demographic determinism— i.e., that simply through the normal replacement of the older generation of Koreans (who tend to have more favorable attitudes) with new generations of better-educated Koreans (who have less favorable attitudes), we can expect further erosion in attitudes toward the U.S.—there are serious reasons for concern that this could be taking place, and policymakers will need to monitor this question closely.

Recommendations

In consultation with our advisory group, we developed six recommendations for U.S. policymakers:

- First, the U.S. should explore opportunities for even more robust intelligence sharing, consultations, and other mechanisms that could help to harmonize U.S.-South Korean views on threats, and appropriate responses. Our view was that the more both parties share a common picture of threats, the easier it will be to harmonize public statements and policies, and avoid perceived divisions that might be exploited by North Korea.[1]

- Second, the U.S. needs to do more now to persuade South Koreans that its interest in the region goes well beyond the North Korean threat, and that it has a long-term interest in a peaceful, stable, and economically vital Northeast Asia. While the outcome of North Korea's efforts to preserve its regime and forestall a collapse cannot be foreseen with any clarity, it is important that South Koreans begin to consider the role of the U.S. in the region following the collapse of the regime in Pyongyang, or reunification.

- Third, the U.S. Government should develop a larger public diplomacy strategy for South Korea that focuses on the legitimate grievances of those who criticize the U.S. (*pimi*), and not attempt to change the views of those whose anti-Americanism (*panmi*) is ideological, and more deeply rooted. The U.S. can, for example, highlight its support for South Korea's participation in the six-party talks on North Korea's nuclear capabilities, which could soften long-standing grievances that the U.S. does not take South Korean interests into account. To the maximum extent possible, the strategy should be a joint U.S.-South Korean one; the No Gun Ri commission might serve as a possible template.

- Fourth, the U.S. should work to better understand the extent to which (if at all) South Korea's educational system constitutes a structural source of anti-American sentiment. It would be useful for the U.S. and South Korea to jointly sponsor surveys and studies that: (1) begin tracking the attitudes of South Korean youths age 13-18 on an annual basis; and (2) content analyze teaching curricula, including textbooks, syllabi and course notes,[2] the teaching methods used, teachers' incentives and other factors that might be encouraging anti-American sentiment. Foundations also might sponsor

---

[1] As the Russian and Chinese threats have diminished, and as South Koreans increasingly view the threat from the north with less alarm, what may really be needed is a new long-term vision for the alliance. We are grateful to Gi-Wook Shin for suggesting this point. For some thoughts on the agenda for the development of such a vision, see Treverton, Larson, and Kim (2003).

[2] One model for such an effort is Linton (1988).

these sorts of studies. The U.S. Government also should (3) evaluate the potential contributions of educational exchange programs, including the Fulbright English Teaching Assistants (ETA) program.

- Fifth, the U.S. needs to better understand the role of the South Korean media in shaping attitudes toward the U.S. and should conduct or commission content analyses of South Korean media reporting on the U.S. and possibly of popular culture, such as music, television, and film.

Our final recommendation is that the U.S. simply should not give up on Korea or Koreans: their attitudes toward the U.S. are quite complex, and in spite of the recent downturn many measures have remained consistently and strongly positive. It remains very much in the U.S. interest to find ways to strengthen these attitudes, while also seeking ways to avoid predictable friction that may arise as a result of perceived slights.[3] And given South Koreans' increasing desire that their preferences and interests be fully considered on bilateral matters—especially dealings with North Korea—the U.S. will need to ensure a much higher level of bilateral coordination on policy matters if further rancor, and crystallization in unfavorable attitudes toward the U.S., are to be avoided.

Conclusions

As described in this report, South Koreans face a changing tableau of positive and negative images and messages from and about the U.S. and the U.S.-South Korean relationship, including the security alliance, trade, economic, and cultural relations, and its other facets, all filtered through the legacy of a complicated and at times tumultuous past, and hopes for a better future. When considering the longer term, uncertainties about the prospects for continued economic growth, reunification, the future shape of Northeast Asia, and South Korea's need for U.S. forces and the alliance introduce notes of caution, and stability, in Koreans' attitudes toward the U.S. The result is a kaleidoscopic image or mosaic of the U.S. that harbors both appreciation, and a desire to see a future South Korea that is a more independent and equal partner.

---

[3]Although we viewed our mandate as working with the members of our advisory group to fashion recommendations, we note that both of our reviewers felt that more forceful recommendations also were possible. One recommended that the following actions be taken: more forthright responses should be made during times of crisis than those that followed the deaths of the schoolgirls; establishment of a hot line; better coordination and planning when announcing major shifts in policy such as the move of U.S. forces south of the Han River; and creation, through the appointment by the Secretaries of Defense and State, of a senior policy advisory group. One of the members of our advisory group strongly endorsed the creation of a policy advisory group that could advise the government on policy toward North Korea, which has been particularly susceptible to diverging approaches.

This basic ambivalence about the United States, which reflects South Koreans' efforts to balance their appreciation of the benefits that flow from a close relationship with the U.S. against continued aspirations arising from national pride and identity, imbues some South Korean attitudes toward the U.S. with a mercurial quality that can, at times, be breathtaking. But as described in this study, if the magnitude of the changes at times seem out of proportion to their proximate causes, the basic direction of the responses are frequently predictable, and even avoidable. The challenge will be to ensure that South Koreans continue to have every reason to believe that the destinies of Koreans and Americans are intertwined, and that this is, in the final analysis, a very good thing.

Bibliography

"Address by President Kim Young-Sam of Korea at a Joint Session of the U.S. Congress," July 26, 1995.

"Anti-U.S. Cyber Campaign' Brisk in South Korea," Korean Central News Agency, April 4, 2002.

"Candlelight Demonstrations Are Energy for Peace," *The Hankyoreh*, December 30, 2002.

"Cyber Protesters Urge ROKG To 'Not Choose' F-15s Over Olympic Disqualification," Yonhap, February 22, 2002.

"Even the President-Elect Is Appealing for Restraining of Demonstrations," *Dong-A Ilbo*, December 30, 2002.

"Even the President-Elect is Appealing for Restraining of Demonstrations," *Dong-A Ilbo*, December 30, 2002.

"Importance of Korea-U.S. Alliance; Closer Cooperation Needed to Cope With Nuclear Crisis," *The Korea Times*, December 30, 2002.

"Joint U.S.-DPRK Press Statement, Kuala Lumpur, June 13, 1995," available online at http://www.kedo.org.

"Korea's Newspaper Readership Lowest Among OECD Nations," Yonhap, October 22, 2003.

"Korea-U.S. Joint Announcement Between Presidents Kim Young-Sam and Bill Clinton," April 16, 1996.

"North Korea's Response," *The New York Times*, October 26, 2002.

"Official Says ROKG Not 'Seriously' Concerned About 'Eruption' of Anti-American Sentiment on 10 June," *The Korea Times*, June 6, 2002.

"President Kim Young-Sam's Speech to the National Assembly on the APEC Leaders Meeting and His Visit to the United States," in Yonhap News Agency Staff, *Korea Annual 1994*, Seoul, Korea: Western Publications Service, 1994, pp. 348-350.

"ROK Daily Polls Public Views on US Relations, ROK President," *Hankook Ilbo*, June 9, 2003, accessed via at FBIS KPP20030609000060, June 20, 2003.

"ROK Media Leaders Worry 'Intense' Anti-Americanism, Call for 'Closer' ROK-US Ties," *The Korea Times*, January 9, 2003.

"ROK President Calls on Cabinet to 'Discuss Ways' to Revise SOFA, Stresses USFK's Role," Yonhap, December 3, 2002.

"ROK President Calls on Soccer Fans for 'Decent' Behavior During ROK-U.S. Match," *The Korea Times*, June 8, 2002.

"ROK President Says Recent Poll Showed Public's Opposition to USFK Withdrawal," *Chosun Ilbo*, January 8, 2003.

"ROK President-Elect Calls for End to Anti-U.S. Candlelight Vigils," Yonhap, December 28, 2002.

"ROK President-elect Calls for End to Anti-U.S. Candlelight Vigils," Yonhap, December 28, 2002.

"Running Against America," *JoongAng Ilbo*, December 7, 2002.

"Statement by Assistant of Secretary of State for East Asian and Pacific Affairs James A. Kelly," October 19, 2002, available at http://usembassy.state.gov/seoul.

"Text of Presidents Kim Young-Sam and Bill Clinton at the Joint Press Conference, *Korea Annual 1994*, pp. 352-353.

"The Elders Speak Out," *JoongAng Ilbo*, January 18, 2003.

Cable News Network, "U.S. 'May Withdraw From South Korea'", Cable News Network, March 6, 2003, online at <http://www.cnn.com>.

Acheson, Dean *Present at the Creation*, The New American Library, Inc., 1970.

Allen, Richard C., *Korea's Syngman Rhee*, Boston: Charles E. Tuttle Company, 1960.

Armacost, Michael H., *Where Are We Today: A Geopolitical Overview*, an unpublished keynote speech given at the Fourth International Symposium on Korea and the Search for Peace in Northeast Asia, Kyoto, Japan, November 18, 2001.

Baik, Seonhae, and Eric Larson, "South Korean Attitudes Toward the U.S.: Public Opinion Data," forthcoming.

Borton, Hugh, *Japan's Modern Century*, New York: The Ronald Press Company, 1970.

Brody, Richard A., *Assessing the President*, Stanford: Stanford University Press, 1992.

Brooke, James, "When American Villains Thwart Lovesick Koreans," *The New York Times*, October 12, 2002.

Brown, David G., "Never Better!... But Can It Last?" *Comparative Connections*, 4th Quarter 1999, online at http://www.csis.org/pacfor.

Bush, George W., "The President's State of the Union Address," January 29, 2002, online at http://www.whitehouse.gov.

Carter, Ashton B. and William J. Perry, *Preventive Defense*, Washington, D.C.: Brookings Institution Press, 1999.

Chae-yong, Chong, "Meaning of President Kim's Comment on SOFA," Yonhap, December 3, 2002.

Chong-mu, Yi, "Pomdaewi's Gathering Methods Do Not Appeal to General Masses? – 50/50 – Results of Pomdaewi's Candlelight [Vigil] Survey," *Voice of People*, January 7, 2003.

Chong-won, Kim, "Commentary on Current Affairs," *Chosun Ilbo*, December 17, 2002.

Clark, Donald N., "Bitter Friendship: Understanding Anti-Americanism in South Korea," in Donald N. Clark, Ed., *Korea Briefing, 1991*, Boulder, CO: Westview, 1991, pp. 147–167.

Conroy, Hilary, *The Japanese Seizure of Korea: 1868–1910*, Philadelphia: University of Pennsylvania Press, 1960.

Cossa, Ralph A., "Trials, Tribulations, Threats, and Tirades," *Comparative Connections*, 4th Quarter 2002, online at http://www.csis.org/pacfor.

Cummings, Bruce, *The Origins of the Korean War: Liberation and the Emergence of Separate Regimes, 1945–1947*, Vol. 1, Princeton, NJ: Princeton University Press, 1990.

Deguervian, Carlos, "Popular ROK Girl Trio Use Anti-American Theme in New Music Video," *The Korea Herald*, March 8, 2002.

Eberstadt, Nicholas N., "Korea," *Strategic Asia 2002-03*, Washington, D.C.: American Enterprise Institute, 2002.

Efron, Sonni, and Mark Magnier, "Rumsfeld May Reduce Forces in South Korea; Talk of Redepoyment Appears to Arise from anti-Americanism in Host Country and Bases' Exposure to Attack by North or Other Foes," *The Los Angeles Times*, February 14, 2003, p. A3.

Faiola, Anthony, "Kicking Up the Dust of History: China Makes Novel Claim to Ancient Kingdom, and Both Koreas Balk," *The Los Angeles Times*, January 22, 2004, p. A15.

Fairbank, John K. , Edwin O. Reischauer, Albert M. Craig, *East Asia: The Modern Transformation*, Boston, Mass: Houghton Mifflin Company, 1965.

French, Howard, "Online Newspaper Shakes Up Korean Politics," *The New York Times*, March 6, 2003.

Gallup International, "Gallup International End of Year Poll 1999," press release, undated (polling in November-December 1999), online at http://www.gallup-international.com/surveys.htm.

128

_____., "Gallup International End of Year Poll 2000," press release, undated (polling in November-December 2000), online at http://www.gallup-international.com/surveys.htm.

_____., "Gallup International End of Year Poll 2001," press release, undated (polling in November-December 2001), online at http://www.gallup-international.com/surveys.htm.

_____., "Gallup International End of Year Poll 2002," press release, undated (polling in November-December 2002), online at http://www. gallup-international.com/surveys.htm.

_____., "Gallup International Iraq Poll 2003," press release, undated (polling in January 2003), online at http://www.gallup-international.com/ surveys.htm.

_____., "Updated and revised Press Release (13th May); New Gallup International Post War Iraq Poll—Global Opinion from 45 countries," press release, May 13, 2003, online at http://www.gallup-international. com/ surveys.htm.

_____., "Gallup International poll on terrorism in the US," press release, undated (polling in September 2001), online at http://www.gallup-international.com/surveys.htm.

_____., "Gallup International poll on terrorism," press release, undated (polling in November-December 2001), online at http://www.gallup-international.com/surveys.htm.

Garten, Jeffrey, "Clinton's Emerging Trade Policy: Act One, Scene One," *Foreign Affairs*, Summer 1993, online at http://www.foreignaffairs.org.

Gross, Donald G., "Riding the Roller-Coaster," *Comparative Connections*, 1st Quarter, 2002, online at http://www.csis.org/pacfor.

Han, Sung-Joo, *The Failure of Democracy in South Korea*, Berkeley, Calif: University of California Press, 1974.

Han, Woo-keun, *The History of Korea*, Honolulu, Hawaii: University of Hawaii Press, 1974.

Henderson, Gregory, *Korea: The Politics of the Vortex*, Cambridge, Mass.: Harvard University Press, 1968.

Ho-t'aek, Hwang, "Emotional Anti-Americanism," *Dong-A Ilbo*, March 26, 2002.

Hyong-ki, Kim, "'007 Boycott' Campaign," *Chosun Ilbo*, January 23, 2003.

"We Have Been Heard," *JoongAng Ilbo*, December 30, 2002.

Hyundai Research Institute, *Survey of South Korean Attitudes Toward National Security; Citizens in General*, survey report for the Security Issues Research Institute, Korea National Defense University, Seoul, Korea, August 14, 2003.

Hyung Jin, Kim, "Parliamentary session paralyzed after MDP lawmaker lambasted opposition leader Lee," *Korea Herald*, February 19, 2002.

Ipsos-Insight, "The Global Internet Population Continues to Grow," press release, January 21, 2004.

Kagay, Michael R., "Variability Without Fault: Why Even Well-Designed Polls Can Disagree," in Thomas E. Mann and Gary R. Orren, Eds., *Media Polls in American Politics*, Washington, D.C.: Brookings, 1992, pp. 95-124.

Kim, Jinwung, "Recent Anti-Americanism in South Korea: The Causes," *Asian Survey*, Vol. 29, No. 8, 1989, pp. 749-753.

Kim, Seung-hwan, "Anti-Americanism in Korea (II)," *The Korea Times*, December 9, 2002.

Kim, Sung-han, "Anti-American Sentiment and the ROK-US Alliance," *Korean Journal of Defense Analysis*, Vol. XV, No. 2, Fall 2003, pp. 105-130.

Kim, Yongho, "Inconsistency or Flexibility? The Kim Young Sam Government's North Korea Policy and its Domestic Variants," *International Journal of Korean Unification Studies*, Vol. 8, 1999.

Kyong-Dong, Kim, "Korean Perceptions of America," in Donald N. Clark, Ed., *Korea Briefing, 1993; Festival of Korea*, Boulder, Colo: Westview, 1993, pp. 163-184.

Larson, Eric V., "An Analysis of the September 2003 *JoongAng Ilbo*-CSIS-RAND Polls of South Korean Attitudes Toward the U.S.," forthcoming in an as-yet untitled volume to be published by the Center for Strategic and International Studies, Washington, D.C.

Lee, Jae-Kyoung, "Anti-Americanism in South Korea: The Media and the Politics of Signification," PhD dissertation, University of Iowa, 1993.

Levin, Norman D. , and Yong-Sup Han, *Sunshine in Korea*, Santa Monica, Calif: RAND Corporation, 2002.

Levin, Norman D., *Do the Ties Still Bind? The U.S.-ROK Security Relationship After 9/11*, Santa Monica, Calif: RAND Corporation, MG-115-AF-KF, forthcoming.

Linton, Stephen, *Coverage of the United States in Korean Textbooks*, Seoul and Washington, D.C.: United States Information Service print, 1988.

Nahm, Andrew C., "U.S. Policy and the Japanese Annexation of Korea," in Tae-Hwan Kwak, et al., (ed.), *U.S-Korean Relations, 1882–1982*, Kyungnam, Korea: Kyungnam University Press, 1982.

Neuman, W. Russell, *The Paradox of Mass Politics: Knowledge and Opinion in the American Electorate*, Cambridge, Mass.: Harvard University Press, 1986.

Niksch, Larry A., "Korea: U.S.-South Korean Relations – Issues for Congress," *Issue Brief for Congress, Updated June 19, 2002*, Washington, D.C.: Congressional Research Service, 2002.

Noerper, Stephen, "Looking Forward, Looking Back," *Comparative Connections,* 2nd Quarter, 2000, online at http://www.csis.org/pacfor.

Oberdorfer, Don, *The Two Koreas,* New York: Basic Books, 2001.

Oliver, Robert T., *Syngman Rhee and American Involvement in Korea, 1942–1960,* Seoul, Korea: Panmun Book Company LTD, 1978.

Omestad, Thomas, "Crisis? What Crisis?" *U.S. News and World Report,* February 17, 2003.

Page, Benjamin I., and Robert Y. Shapiro, *The Rational Public: Fifty Years of Trends in Americans' Policy Preferences,* Chicago, Ill: University of Chicago Press, 1992.

Pew Center for People and the Press, "What the World Thinks in 2002; How Global Publics View: Their Lives, Their Countries, The World, America," Washington, D.C., December 4, 2002.

_____., "Views of a Changing World 2003; War With Iraq Further Divides Global Publics," Washington, D.C., June 3, 2003.

_____., "International Public Concern About North Korea; But Growing Anti-Americanism in South Korea," press release, August 22, 2003.

_____., "Cable and Internet Loom Large in Fragmented Political Universe," Washington, D.C., January 11, 2004.

Pu-kun, An, "Poll Shows More Support for Military Ties With US," *JoongAng Ilbo,* June 12, 2003, accessed via FBIS KPP20030612000008, August 25, 2003.

Pyong-kyu, Yi, "Anti-American Sentiment is Crossing the Line," *Hankook Ilbo,* February 28, 2002.

Risse, Nicole, "The Evolution in anti-Americanism in South Korea: From Ideologically Embedded to Socially Constructed," KSAA CONFERENCE paper, September 24, 2001.

ROK Ministry of National Defense, *ROK-US Alliance and USFK,* Seoul, Korea: Ministry of National Defense, 2002.

ROK Ministry of National Unification, *Peace and Cooperation—White Paper on Korean Unification 1996,* Seoul: Ministry of National Unification, 1996.

Sang-chu, Pak, "Anti-U.S. [Sentiment] in Red Devil Generation," *Munhwa Ilbo,* December 3, 2002 [2002a].

_____, "Presidential Candidates Cautiously Ride Anti-U.S. Sentiments," Yonhap, December 6, 2002 [2002b].

_____, "Running Against America," *JoongAng Ilbo,* December 7, 2002 [2002c].

Savych, Bogdan, and Eric Larson, "South Korean Attitudes Toward the U.S.: Statistical Modeling Results," forthcoming.

Shin, Doh Chull, Chong-Min Park, and Jiho Jang, *The Growth of Democratic Political Sophistication in Korea*, Glasgow, Scotland: University of Strathclyde, Studies in Public Policy No. 369, 2002.

Shin, Gi-Wook, "Marxism, Anti-Americanism, and Democracy in South Korea: An Examination of Nationalist Intellectual Discourse," *Positions: East Asia Cultures Critique*, Vol. 3, No. 2, 1995, pp. 508-534.

Shin, Gi-Wook, "South Korean Anti-Americanism: A Comparative Perspective," *Asian Survey*, Vol. 36, No. 8, 1996, pp. 787-803.

Shorrock, Tim, "The Struggle for Democracy in South Korea in the 1980s and the Rise of Anti-Americanism," *Third World Quarterly*, Vol. 8, No. 4, 1986, pp. 1195-1218.

Siddons, Larry, "Golden Ohno: Korean Protest Dismissed by Arbitration Panel," Associated Press, February 23, 2002.

Sigal, Leon V., *Disarming Strangers: Nuclear Diplomacy with North Korea*, Princeton, NJ: Princeton University Press, 1998.

Snyder, Scott, *Negotiating on the Edge*, Washington, D.C.: United States Institute of Peace Press, 1999

Sterngold, James, "South Korea President Lashes Out at U.S.," *New York Times*, October 8, 1994.

T'ae-hyon, Kwak, "President No Says at Luncheon With Veterans Association Executives, 'USFK Will Not Stay for 10 or 20 Years,'," *Taehan Maeil*, October 18, 2003.

Tae Chung, Kim, "Anti-American Sentiment and Anti-Americanism," *Seoul Chosun Ilbo*, October 21, 2002.

Tae-chung, Kim, "Anti-Americanism," *Chosun Ilbo*, October 22, 2002.

T'ae-kyong, Song, "GNP to Woo Young Voters Online," *The Korea Times*, July 28, 2003.

Taylor, Humphrey, "Attitudes to United States, Japan and China in U.S. and Seven Asian Countries, The Harris Poll #66, November 10, 1999, online at http://www.harrisinteractive.com/harris_poll/

Treverton, Gregory F., Eric V. Larson, and Spencer H. Kim, "Bridging the 'Open Water' in the US-South Korea Military Alliance," *The Korean Journal of Defense Analysis*, Vol. XV, No. 2, Fall 2003, pp. 153-176.

U.S. Department of Defense, *Nuclear Posture Review*, Washington, D.C.: January 8, 2002

Watts, William, *Next Generation Leaders in the Republic of Korea: Opinion Survey Report and Analysis*, Washington, D.C., Potomac Associates, April 2002.

Wickham, John A., *Korea on the Brink*, Dulles, VA: Brassey's, 2000.

132

Yong-chin, O, "Roh Warns Against Anti-American Lessons," *The Korea Times*, April 30, 2003.

Young-shik, Yang, "Kim Dae-Jung Administration's North Korea Policy," *Korea Focus*, November-December 1998, pp. 54-55.

Zaller, John R., *The Nature and Origins of Mass Opinion*, Cambridge: Cambridge University Press, 1992.